"These thirty-one short readings will scoot you up to the banquet table of God's grace and glory and leave you feasting on your Savior and the cross. But beware: this cross-centered diet will change the way you live. Get ready for joy, power, contentment, security, and hope to flood your life as you sink your teeth into this feast. These short meditations will shape your heart and mind. We need this book! The church today, particularly in America, has been languishing in selfish, impotent, shallow immaturity—barely able to survive, let alone thrive and make an impact on our culture. So this book is a gem that stands out in the mountain of Christian self-help, feel-good, and name-it-and-claim-it books that have dominated the Christian landscape for too long. Get this book. Read it, and give it away to someone else who needs a gospel booster shot."

> —BRAD BIGNEY, Senior Pastor, Grace Fellowship Church, Florence, Kentucky

"The love of God in its deepest intensity is found in the immediate vicinity of the cross, and this is where Elyse invites her readers to dwell for thirty-one days of gospel meditation. Poignant and thoroughly biblical, *Comforts from the Cross* presents an endearing view of Christ that will encourage Christians with a fresh hope in their Savior. This book also provides a wide-ranging tour of gospel truths and shows readers how to apply them with life-changing results. This book is truly a gift to women who want their lives to bear more deeply the imprint of God's love."

> —MILTON VINCENT, author, *A Gospel Primer for Christians*

D0874366

Comforts from the Cross

Comforts from the Cross

– Celebrating the Gospel One Day at a Time –

Elyse M. Fitzpatrick

CROSSWAY BOOKS
WHEATON, ILLINOIS

Comforts from the Cross: Celebrating the Gospel One Day at a Time

Copyright © 2009 by Elyse M. Fitzpatrick

Published by Crossway Books
    a publishing ministry of Good News Publishers
    1300 Crescent Street
    Wheaton, Illinois 60187

Cover design: The DesignWorks Group, www.thedesignworksgroup.com

Cover photo: iStock

First printing 2009

Printed in the United States of America

PDF ISBN: 978-1-4335-0555-3

Mobipocket ISBN: 978-1-4335-0556-0

Library of Congress Cataloging-in-Publication Data
Fitzpatrick, Elyse, 1950–
   Comforts from the cross : celebrating the gospel on day at a
time / Elyse Fitzpatrick.
     p. cm.
   ISBN 978-1-4335-0283-5 (tpb)
   1. fChristian women—Religious life. 2. Bible N.T.—Meditations.
I. Title
BV4527.F583   2009
242'.2—dc22   2008053282

VP		18	17	16	15	14	13	12	11	10	09
14	13	12	11	10	9	8	7	6	5	4	3	2	1

To Laura
A sweet sister with a Little name
And a great love for our Savior.

Contents

Acknowledgments

This book was originally the idea of my dear friend Laura Little (now Gannon). Thanks, Laura. I hope you'll find comfort here. I have the great privilege to bask continually in the glowing light of the gospel. I'm blessed to hear strong, Christ-centered preaching every Sunday. Our senior pastor, Mark Lauterbach, along with Dan Wilson and Eric Turbedsky have the earthly care of my soul and regularly drench me with the gospel. Much of what you read here is a result of Mark's preaching. Thank you, Mark.

My friends love the gospel and remind me of it constantly. Rondi Lauterbach carefully read every "celebration" and offered gentle, helpful correction. My friends Donna, Anita, Cherie, Jessica, Kei, Laura L., Laura H., Chelsea, Aaron and Monica, and Glenn and Laura C. read and rejoiced with me. My heart is so bent towards self-righteousness, pride, laziness, and despair. Thank you for making me remember Jesus. My small group probed and pushed and loved me when I wanted to retreat to a cave and be left alone. And they ate the dinners I prepared and acted like they were delicious. Thank you all.

My family waits and encourages. My husband Phil loves me and is my greatest source of earthly comfort. My children love their mother and have given me six delectable grandchildren to delight in. I've been so blessed.

Lydia Brownback and Allan Fisher from Crossway understand the gospel and want to spread the message. They're pouring out their lives for the sake of the church, and they've been another great source of earthly encouragement to me.

Thank you all. Celebrate with me. We're so blessed.

Introduction

I love celebrations. I love parties and getting together with friends and Christmas trees and water slides in the front yard. I love barbeques and Thanksgiving and birthday candles and having our church small group over for dinner and fellowship. The Lord has blessed my husband, Phil, and me with the perfect party house and "the more, the merrier" is our motto. There's something intrinsically wonderful about being with others around a shared joy, isn't there? Give me a birthday party or any holiday party and a houseful of guests and I'm in my element. I know that this kind of ruckus drives some people batty. Not me, I thrive on it. In fact, one of the dearest thoughts of heaven to me is the marriage supper of the Lamb. Sounds like a party. I can't wait.

Through this book I'm inviting you to join me in a month's worth of daily "celebrations." These celebrations won't center on temporal fetes like birthdays or national holidays or even the Mad Hatter's "Un-birthday." Instead, they're all about Jesus Christ: his incarnation, sinless life, substitutionary death, bodily resurrection, ascension, and ongoing reign as Lord of all there is. In other words, we're going to be celebrating the gospel.

I'm assuming that right about now you might be wondering why you would need to celebrate the gospel every day. You might think you already know it; in fact, I'm pretty sure that most of you do. Most of you would be able to clearly articulate the facts of Jesus' birth, death, and resurrection. But this book isn't about mere facts, although these facts are true and significant. This book is about how those facts are to inform, free, gladden, and enliven your soul every day—when you're struggling to balance the checkbook, stuck in traffic or in a hospital bed, or just bored with the same-old-same-old. These facts are so much more than mere facts, and yet, the longer we walk with God, the more likely we are to forget about them. Here's my perspective: nothing, and I mean *nothing*, is more important than Jesus Christ and the gospel, and this gospel is meant to be remembered and celebrated *every day*.

So, here's your invitation: join me for the next month, won't you? I'm praying that the Spirit will use our time together to comfort, transform, and encourage you as we revisit ancient realities and dust off the truths that once enflamed our hearts with first love.

(Oh, by the way, if you're not sure that you're a Christian, I've included a short summary of this really great news in Appendix 1. You can turn there now before you start reading, so that you'll understand what I mean when I talk about being a Christian. Thanks!)

Day 1

Celebrate Jesus

*As often as you eat this bread and drink the cup, you proclaim
the Lord's death until he comes.*

1 CORINTHIANS 11:26

Once a month, usually on the first Sunday, we celebrate communion in our church. Our pastor frequently quotes this familiar passage from 1 Corinthians:

> For I received from the Lord what I also delivered to you, that the Lord Jesus on the night when he was betrayed took bread, and when he had given thanks, he broke it, and said, "This is my body which is for you. Do this in remembrance of me." In the same way also he took the cup, after supper, saying, "This cup is the new covenant in my blood. Do this, as often as you drink it, in remembrance of me." For as often as you eat this bread and drink the cup, you proclaim the Lord's death until he comes. (1 Cor. 11:23–26)

Communion is given to us to help us remember Jesus, and I, for one, am glad. I'm glad because it's so easy for me to forget him. I forget his betrayal at night, his unfeigned gratitude while the crushing jaws of judgment were irresistibly gaping before him. His blood flowed and yet he bent before his friends and washed their feet. I forget that he's reigning right now as the sovereign Lord and that soon he'll shatter the heavens and come for me. I forget all those truths, but the communion service helps me remember them.

In a similar way, I'm reminding you today: celebrate Jesus. Although it might seem absurd to tell Christians that we need to remember him, it's my conviction that none of us thinks nearly enough about him and what he's done. We don't consider how the gospel—the good news about him—is meant to affect every facet of our day-to-day life.

If you are like me, perhaps the name of Jesus does cross your mind, usually as a prayer shot up in haste when the freeway is a parking lot or the parking lot is as jammed as a rush-hour freeway. Does it seem as though the story of Christ's life, death, and resurrection are cherished truths yet strangely disconnected from daily life? Are they kind of like your elderly aunt's jewels that are kept in a safe deposit box at the bank? You know they are there and that you could see them any time you asked, but they aren't part of your everyday life, and you never think about them unless you're in a jam and wonder if she might let you pawn a piece or two. No, our thoughts are generally entangled with baseball tryouts, melted crayons in the dryer, and the silence around the dinner table now that the kids have moved out.

Jesus? Oh yes, I remember Jesus, but right now I'm trying to figure out why my future seems so bleak and why my friends seem to be unconcerned about my loneliness. I just don't see how his death and imminent return make much difference. In the way we speak to our children when they disappoint, the way we celebrate special holidays, the attitude we embrace when our fondest hopes are dashed, the prayer we utter when physical pain engulfs us, we're to proclaim his death until he comes back for us. But how can we do that?

We do that by intentionally focusing our thought on him instead of on ourselves or on what we think we're missing. I think it's very easy for me to focus my attention on myself. I don't mean that I just sit around thinking about me and how wonderful I am (although I'm not above that!). No, I mean that I tend to focus my thought on my Christianity—how I'm doing, what I'm learning, how my prayer time was today, how I avoided that pesky sin or fell into it again. I think about what I'm supposed to accomplish for Christ, and I interact with others on that same works-oriented ground. But this day isn't about me at all. It's about him: his sinless life, death, resurrection, ascension, and reign and the sure promise of his return. It's the gravity of his life that should attract my thought toward him.

Plainly stated, let me encourage you to proclaim the gospel to yourself today and every day. Our poor burdened hearts are in such need of a gospel celebration. When you fail today, you need the comfort of this proclamation: he died for that very sin. Tell yourself about his death. When you feel overwhelmed by your responsibilities, remember that he is ruling sovereignly over every facet of your life, and soon he will return to right every wrong and relieve you of your trouble. When you wonder if your life will ever change, he wants you to remember that he is coming back and that this life as it is won't last forever. Make a proclamation! Celebrate! "I'm forgiven; he's paid the penalty for all my sin; he's my husband, and soon he'll return to take me to our heavenly home!" You might pray:

Lord,

Cause me to live this day proclaiming your death and your soon return— to others, yes, but also to myself. Although it seems as though I'm going to drown under my burdens, help me to see you ruling powerfully from heaven. You will come for me and save me completely. I can trust that you'll do this because you've shown me your love by dying in my place. Help me understand how to connect the dots between your death and return and my day today.

AMEN

Day 2

No More Wrath

*For the law brings wrath, but where there is no law
there is no transgression.*

ROMANS 4:15

Although my memory is pretty hazy at this point, I do very clearly
remember a day when, as a child, my older brother found me
playing outdoors and warned, "You're really in trouble. You'd better
get home right away." Although I can't recall what I did that prompted
this warning, even today some fifty years later, I do remember how I
felt: afraid, uncomfortable, guilty. Of course, that scenario has been
repeated thousands of times since then. I'll admit that I've frequently
felt much the same way as an adult, yes, even as a Christian—like
someone was mad at me and I was about to be punished. I'm assuming it's the same for you.

Yesterday I encouraged you to proclaim Christ's death to yourself;
during the times when you experience lingering guilt or anticipation
of punishment you especially need to do just that. To stimulate your
thinking, here are a few simple questions: Do you think God gets mad
at you? Can you picture him saying, "You're really in trouble now!"?
Do you think he's a demanding, impatient, angry Father just waiting
for an opportunity to punish you? If you answered yes to any of those
questions, you need the comfort that only the gospel can bring, and
for that comfort we'll look to the book of Romans.

Here's an amazing statement, "For the law brings wrath, but

where there is no law there is no transgression" (4:15). The reason that I continue to experience guilt, shame, and fear is that I've been a lawbreaker all my life. We all know what it's like to live with—and break—laws and rules. My mom told me when to be home and how to make my bed. The government tells me how fast to drive. Books tell me how to communicate with my husband and how to raise my children. And of course, the Bible tells all of us what God commands. We live in a world governed by laws. The Bible tells us that God's law is good, but we have a problem with it. Even as Christians we don't obey it perfectly, and so day after day we live with guilt and fear of punishment.

Here's a gospel truth that is just astounding and meant to comfort your guilty, burdened soul: because Jesus Christ perfectly obeyed every facet of the law in your place and then died bearing all the guilt and wrath that was rightfully yours, you are no longer obligated to obey the law as a way to avoid his wrath. God has already poured out every drop of his wrath on his Son in your place. You are no longer subject to wrath, because wrath is the result of transgression or sin, and sins can be committed only when there is a law that has been violated. So now, if you're in Christ, *there is no law that you can break that will bring God's punitive wrath upon you*, or, as Paul put it, "Where there is no law there is no transgression," and hence, no "wrath." No wrath for you because you're in Christ, and God has no wrath left for him. No wrath. Not ever.

Do you believe that there is no wrath left for you? That once you are God's, it is impossible for you to receive his judgment? Do you believe that the darkness of your sin will never be powerful enough to snuff out the light of his grace? Do you understand that all he requires of you is to believe this truth? You must believe that the gospel story is true not just for others but personally for you. Do you believe that God is good enough and powerful enough to conquer all your sin and irreversibly love you?

Faith is all that is necessary. However, not only is faith necessary for your salvation, but it's also necessary for your ongoing obedience. Responding to his love and grace is the only way to true or what I call "gospelized" obedience, because all other obedience *always* degenerates into penance or trying to avoid punishment. Other forms of obedience simply don't measure up, because love for God isn't the motive. And if love isn't the motive, your obedience will always be motivated by love for yourself. It seems upside down to say that God motivates our obedience by freeing us from law and by declaring that he has no wrath left for us, but it's true, and true faith embraces it.

To help you understand this principle, let me ask you a few more questions: How do you act when you feel guilty? How do you feel about someone you might have offended? Does your guilt make you love him more? Of course not. When I feel guilty, it isn't long before I'm comparing my behavior with my accuser's, feeling angry or self-justifying, or spending hours in self-recrimination and despair. Guilt doesn't produce love; only grace does that.

Of course, sometimes we feel guilty, and we don't really care that God isn't angry with us. We know we've let our spouse or kids or parents or friends or employer or church or ourselves down, and we just can't seem to get past it. In these times we've got to see that our problem with guilt stems from our pride and from our idolatry of people's opinions. There's only one Person whose opinion really matters, and all the rest of our guilt is just our desire to approve of ourselves and make ourselves happy. Rejoice because your Savior bore even this sin for you.

We're going to spend another twenty-nine days together celebrating the comfort of the gospel, considering how it should transform us, but for now let me leave you with one more verse. Here is Paul again: "Therefore, since we have been justified by faith, we have peace with God through our Lord Jesus Christ" (Rom. 5:1). You've been declared righteous because you believe that the gospel is true, that God is *that* good, and that now he is at peace with you. He's made a peace treaty and turned his good countenance upon you; he'll never be angry with you again.

Why not spend some time in grateful celebration now? Here is a way you might pray:

Father,

Thank you that you have declared your love for me and that nothing, no matter what I do or say today, can dissuade you from that love. Thank you that you've freed me from trying to earn your favor and that you'll never punish me in anger. Thank you that I don't have to worry about measuring up anymore because your Son measured up in my place and bore your wrath for my failure, and now, when you look at me, you see his perfections and say, "This is my beloved daughter, in whom I am well pleased." Please help me celebrate your grace today and respond in grateful obedience for your pleasure and glory.

AMEN

Day 3

Presented in Splendor

*Husbands, love your wives, as Christ loved the church
and gave himself up for her.*

EPHESIANS 5:25

Yesterday I told you that your heavenly Father has no wrath left
for you. He doesn't have any wrath left because he poured out all
of it on his Son. And just in case you think there is a possibility that
you might career into it again, let me remind you that wrath is the
result of breaking the law, and the law no longer applies to you. You
are no longer under obligation to try to obey the law as a way of earn-
ing favor with God, because every demand of the law has been satisfied in Jesus Christ. His frown has been replaced by a smile, by love,
and by an eager anticipation of the day you wed his beloved Son.

In all the kind and loving ways that a devoted groom anticipates his
wedding day, Jesus Christ is anticipating his. Here's how Paul describes
the work Jesus has done in preparation for that celebration:

> Husbands, love your wives, as Christ loved the church and gave
> himself up for her, that he might sanctify her, having cleansed her
> by the washing of water with the word, so that he might present the
> church to himself in splendor, without spot or wrinkle or any such
> thing, that she might be holy and without blemish. (Eph. 5:25–27)

I know that the focus in this verse is usually on the command to
husbands to love their wives, and it's not wrong to use it in that way.

But this verse is not primarily about our earthly husbands. It's about the self-sacrificing love that the Savior has for you, his bride. Listen to what he's done and how he thinks of you.

He determined to love you and so gave himself up for you. He fell as a sinner (though he was innocent) into the hands of the living God. Consider the power of the love that motivated him to intentionally plunge himself into a fiery furnace that burned with relentless wrath, bearing in a few short hours an infinity of hellish misery. He bore intense suffering in his body and soul so that he would be granted the right to have you, a redeemed sinner, for his bride. As the Apostles' Creed says, "He descended into hell." He gave himself up to hell so that you might be his delight in heaven, and he was faithful to accomplish his goal.

He has set you apart for his own pleasure, just the same way that an engaged man declares, "This woman is mine, and though we're not actually husband and wife yet, she belongs to me and I to her." But Jesus is not like a modern fiancé, waiting to see his bride in the gown she chose for the wedding day. No, Jesus has taken on the responsibility to dress you beautifully, too. It's his delight to dress you in garments that befit your calling as the bride of the Lord of lords. Here's how the prophet Isaiah describes this transformation:

> He has clothed me with the garments of salvation; he has covered me with the robe of righteousness, as a bridegroom decks himself like a priest with a beautiful headdress, and as a bride adorns herself with her jewels. (Isa. 61:10)

He has clothed you in a "robe of righteousness." He is the priest with a beautiful headdress, and you are the bride adorned with jewels—not just a pretty dress but a gown bejeweled with precious gems interwoven with golden thread. When he looks at you, he smiles with contentment and deep affection. He has cleansed you completely so that you are radiant, without any stain or shadow of guilt or impurity. Your wedding gown is just as it should be: glistening, white, pure.

Even though we may recognize these words as true, I know that it's still a temptation to give in to vain introspection—to examine our record, our accomplishments, our growth—comparing ourselves to others. *Her dress looks prettier than mine. She's always so kind and*

I'm so selfish. The Lord must love her more than he loves me. Then, when we focus too narrowly on our sin, we compound our guilt by hiding from Christ in shame. *I'm sure he's disappointed with me. I dare not come to him. I just hope he doesn't notice how defiled I am.* We're like a bride who insanely shreds her gown because she thinks that other brides are more beautiful and then hides in a corner, ashamed, self-condemning, wretched. All she sees is her shame. She doesn't notice that her dress remains as it always was: beautiful, whole, clean. *But I did that again! But I was selfish and angry!"* is the refrain that resounds in our hearts. This refrain needs to be replaced by a proclamation: Christ has given himself up for our disgrace. His blood has washed away all our impurity. He has completely cleansed us so that we're without spot, wrinkle, or blemish of any kind. No stain, no disgrace, no defect. All our shame is gone, and he declares us to be holy. But that's not all.

He has presented you to himself "in splendor." This is what he thinks when he looks upon his bride: *Isn't she magnificent! She's gorgeous, glorious, noble, honorable.* Think in terms of Princess Diana on her wedding day and then let your imagination soar. That gown, that honor, that glory. That's how he sees you. *Ah, this is my beloved bride. Isn't she beautiful?* he thinks. Are you able to see his adoring smile?

As you face this day and all of the disappointments, failures, and vicissitudes of living life here in this defiled world, think: *He won't fail to present me to himself "in splendor" because it has, in fact, already been accomplished. I feel inadequate, dirty, ashamed. He sees me as being honorable, glorious, noble, magnificently beautiful; filled with splendor through and through because of what he's done.* And remember this: you're not beautiful just because you have been allowed to play dress-up with some other beautiful bride's wardrobe; no, he's made *you* holy—spirit, soul, and body. *Presented in splendor? Me?* Yes, "He who calls you is faithful; he will surely do it" (1 Thess. 5:23–24). We're not playing dress-up. This is who we really are. You might pray:

Father,

Cause me to have faith to believe that you can accomplish even this. Help me to think of myself as a beautiful bride, not as an embarrassment or dis-

grace to you. As I have opportunities to serve you today, help me remember what you've made me to be. In your love you've completely cleansed me and adorned me with jewels and clothed me in a gown woven with threads from your righteous life. Cause me to celebrate the splendor you've bestowed on me today and let me rest in the healing beams of radiant love emanating from your smile.

AMEN

Day 4

Dead to the Law

Likewise, my brothers, you also have died to the law through
the body of Christ, so that you may belong to another,
to him who has been raised from the dead, in order that
we may bear fruit for God.

ROMANS 7:4

It would be ridiculous to walk through a cemetery commanding the bodies in the graves to rise and pay their taxes, wouldn't it? That's because dead people have no obligation to obey the law. People who have died and those who demand compliance to the law have nothing to say to each other. That is the very point that Paul is making in Romans 7.

> Or do you not know, brothers . . . that the law is binding on a person only as long as he lives? For a married woman is bound by law to her husband while he lives, but if her husband dies she is released from the law of marriage. . . . Likewise, my brothers, you also have died to the law through the body of Christ, so that you may belong to another, to him who has been raised from the dead, in order that we may bear fruit for God. (Rom. 7:1–2)

To summarize Paul's point, because we are dead, the law no longer has any power over us. Using the analogy of marriage he writes that our former husband (we'll call him Mr. Law) had power over us as long as we lived, but now that we have died, we are free to marry another. He says that we have "died to the law through the body of Christ." That is, when Jesus Christ died, he didn't die only as a punishment for our sin. He died so that our old husband, Mr. Law, would no longer have a claim on us; when Christ died, we died too. Now that we have really and truly died in his death, we are completely free from our former obligations to Mr. Law. We can freely and joyfully enter into a new marriage to someone else—to Jesus Christ, the one raised from the dead.

Now we're going to change the metaphor a bit. Rather than saying that we have died, I want you to imagine that it is your first husband, Mr. Law, who has died. (Paul uses the metaphor both ways, too.)

Imagine, if you will, losing a spouse in death and then entering into marriage with someone else. It would be understandable if it might take some time to get used to living with your new husband. If your former husband was very demanding and disapproving, it might take even more time to get used to the love and acceptance that your present husband wants to shower upon you. But it certainly won't help you love your new husband if you keep your focus on all your failures in the first marriage. You see, that's Paul's point, exactly. You won't "bear fruit for God" if you continually think about how you have failed to keep the law. Instead, your heart and mind have to be convinced of the love of your new husband, and you have to delight in him alone.

It's only a responsive love for Jesus and all he has done for you personally that will cause godly fruit to be born in your life. To help you understand this point, let me ask you a simple question: In the New Testament, what were the characteristics of the Pharisees, those who prided themselves on their law keeping? Were they bearing fruit for God or were they slaves to the law? What did this duty-driven slavery produce in them? Simply put: it produced envy, hatred, ambition, and unbelief. People who are intent on obeying the law as a way to earn favor with God will *always* end up judging, envying, and hating God and others (Gal. 5:14, 25–26).

It is only responsive love for God in light of what he's done that will engender joyful obedience. The only one who ever obeyed the law perfectly did so because he loved to do the things that were pleasing to his Father. He wasn't trying to make his Father love him; *he knew that his Father already did* (John 3:35; 8:29; 15:10). So, we too, must be assured that he already loves and welcomes us, and then we'll grow in our obedience.

This is why I'm going to remind you to celebrate these truths over and over again. It's not because I'm against obedient living; it's because I long for it. I long for our lives to be filled with delicious, luscious fruit that tastes so good that others are irresistibly drawn to Christ. But the only way your life will produce that kind of fruit will be for you to understand what the law did and continues to do to you. If you still labor under the misconception that obedience to it is the only way he'll love and accept you, your love for him will eventually degenerate into a futile attempt to approve of yourself, resulting in more self-love and despair. You must remember, day after day, until you're perfected in eternity: your husband, Jesus Christ, has severed your relationship with the law.

Paul writes about this in the remainder of Romans 7. (If you have time to read it today, perhaps you should.) He knew that striving to obey the law out of grudging duty will inescapably produce a greater desire to disobey, and disobedience produces death (vv. 5, 8). Even though I know that I should love the law and seek to obey it because it is from God and is therefore good, the sin that lives in my heart persistently causes me to rebel against it (vv. 15–20). The compounding effect of my continued disobedience and rebellion convinces me that God couldn't possibly love me, and because of that I chafe under his commands and give in to self-indulgence and unbelief. *It is utterly impossible that my sinful heart could ever be conquered by anything but God's love and lavish grace.*

It is grace, not law, that enables me to put to death my sinful nature. Paul groans, realizing how entrapped his heart is by sin and the law, and writes, "Wretched man that I am! Who will deliver me from this body of death?" Of course the answer is the only One who could possibly change us: "Thanks be to God through Jesus Christ our Lord!" (Rom. 7:24–25).

Who will deliver us from our wretchedness and death? More rules or seven steps to perfection? No. Only our heavenly husband, Jesus Christ. Ponder this delightful thought as you bring your heart to him now: he has brought you into his bedchamber as his bride, so when law comes pounding on the door, demanding a hearing, accusing you of sin, Jesus answers him: "This woman is my wife now. She is under my care and protection and I love her. Be gone, you vile corpse! She belongs to me and will always be as she is now: completely loved by me!"

Day 5

Cured—and Clean

His disciples said to him,
"You see the crowd pressing around you, and yet you say,
'Who touched me?'"

MARK 5:31

Excluded. Unclean. Defiled. For twelve desperate years she had struggled against her body. Blood poured from her, and that blood not only brought about personal distress but also made her a societal outcast. If she was a married woman, she would have been unable to have sexual relations with her husband. Even if she was precious to him, he could not take her into his arms. Married or single, she was excluded from participation in normal family life. If she had children, she couldn't lie in bed and play with them. Anyone who sat on a chair on which she had sat would be unclean and would have to wash ceremonially and then offer a sacrifice at the temple. When the family went to the temple on a holy day, she had to stay home.

To live in such isolation after childbirth was expected in those days, but the new mother was surrounded by a loving family, all waiting the day when the priest finally declared the mother clean.

But the isolation experienced by the bleeding woman wasn't the usual week or two; it was twelve years. Twelve years without access to worship. Twelve years of gossip whispered behind her back. Mothers would have warned their daughters: "Don't go near; she's unclean."

Twelve years without a caress, a touch, an inviting smile. Twelve years of desperate exclusion, loneliness, and shame.

That she was desperate is clear. She "had suffered much under many physicians, and had spent all that she had" (Mark 5:26). We can imagine that year after year she heard about women in other villages who were cured, so she rushed to uncover their secret, scraping up the necessary payments, yet she "was no better but rather grew worse." Every penny she could get her hands on went to doctors who only exacerbated her condition.

I can't imagine what terrible indignities she suffered at their hands. This wasn't modern medicine with its tidy gynecological offices housing highly trained physicians who write prescriptions for hormonal therapies and perform sanitary procedures. No, ancient medicine consisted of the most base herbal preparations, poultices, and methods that not only failed to cure her but made her suffering worse. She was unclean and her uncleanness had bankrupted her. And still she bled. Days and months of disappointment followed by months and years of shame and isolation. She could touch no one; no one wanted her touch. And now, all hope was gone. She had no money left, so even if a cure could be found, she couldn't afford it.

Then she heard reports about a holy man who loved unclean women and welcomed them as followers. Many had been ill like her. Some had been possessed by devils; others had been notoriously wicked, but he had healed and welcomed them all. Amazingly, hope began to grow within her breast again. Perhaps she thought, *I have no money to pay him. I can't touch him because I'm unclean.* But even so, she believed, "If I touch even his garments, I will be made well" (v. 28). So she waited until his followers and the crowds were passing by, and she slipped into the press. Keeping her head down and her shawl up, she furtively pushed her way ever closer to the One. *There he is. If I can just stretch out my hand past these others! I'm almost there; please don't let me be discovered. There! With my fingertips I brushed his cloak.* Immediately, she felt her body change. The blood stopped. She was healed. The crowd moved on, but she stood still—a whole, clean, honorable woman at last. She had finally received all that she hoped for, but she was soon to learn that her expectation had been far too small.

From the midst of her reverie she noticed the crowd halt. The Master was speaking, "Who touched my garments?" (v. 30). An icy shard of fear pierced her heart. *What if this holy man finds out what I did and takes my healing from me? What if he is angry because I've made him unclean by my touch? Will this simply end in more shame, more separation?* While his disciples pointed out the size of the crowd, the woman bravely made her way to him. In fear and trembling she "fell down before him and told him the whole truth" (v. 33).

How did he respond? He called her "Daughter." This is the only time that Jesus actually called a woman by this name; it was a sweet acknowledgment of relationship and endearment. Instead of pushing her away, he drew her close. *Daughter*—she probably hadn't heard that word in many years. She was a daughter again, and everything that came with the name—relationship, healing, and peace—was restored to her.

Don't be confused. Jesus wasn't stumped about who had touched him. He knew this woman's name (even though we don't). It had been written on his heart for twelve times twelve million years—yes, forever. This woman would have been satisfied with physical healing, but her Savior would not. He forced her to come to him and be in relationship with him, to fall down before him, to come out of the shadows and into the full light of day. Our Savior loves to give us gifts, but the best gift of all is himself, and he won't let us slink off, back into darkness and isolation. No, his love will pull us out of our shame, defilement, and fears, and then he'll speak gently and lovingly to us. "Daughter, be at peace."

Because Jesus is completely pure, he isn't concerned about becoming defiled by touching us. He's not afraid that our uncleanness will contaminate him. Instead he draws us near; he speaks to us in love. He sees our desperation, our bankruptcy, and our uncleanness, and he calls us "Daughter." If you're like me, it's easy to find a measure of satisfaction and peace in knowing that our sins are forgiven and we've been cleansed. But our Savior wants more than that. He's taken us for his bride, and he isn't satisfied when we hide from him or try to use him for our own purposes. Yes, we want to be clean, and he wants that for us too; but clean strangers aren't what he's after. He means to have a wife. And so he continually brings us to points of desperation when we have to fall before him, broken and bankrupt, and then he speaks lovingly to our hearts and draws us up into his presence.

Don't be afraid to go to him now. He isn't fazed by your sin; he isn't afraid that you will contaminate him. In fact, as you get close to him, his holiness will infect you. Go ahead, daughter; press in through the crowd of all that threatens to block access to him—your shame, pride, destitution, and uncleanness. Touch him out of your desperation and find him patiently loving and awaiting your arrival.

Day 6

Silencing the Accuser

And I heard a loud voice in heaven, saying,
"Now the salvation and the power and the kingdom of our God
and the authority of his Christ have come,
for the accuser of our brothers has been thrown down,
who accuses them day and night before our God."

REVELATION 12:10

If you belong to Jesus today, your enemy, Satan, has two goals: to remind you of your sin and to accuse you continually before God. Satan takes perverse pleasure in reminding you over and over again of your failures. He does this to dishonor Jesus Christ and make you turn your eyes in upon yourself in endless over-scrupulousness and introspection. He does this so that you will not love your Savior or have the faith to obey him.

Please don't misunderstand me here. I'm not saying that it is wrong to examine ourselves or ask God to reveal our sin. It is appropriate and good that we allow the Spirit to illumine our hearts to our sin, that we ask others in the body to speak to us and hold us accountable. Because sin is so very deceptive, we need the help of the Spirit and the church.

What I hope you'll avoid, though, is the continual rehearsal over and over again of sins, particularly those you have repented of. Such rehearsal is not a result of the ministry of the Holy Spirit. It is a function of our enemy as he incites our pride. For instance, there are sins in my life that I committed years and years ago, and yet hardly a day goes by without my revisiting them. I would like to think that is because I'm so bent on holiness, but I doubt that's the case. If I were really that concerned about God's honor, I would believe what he has said about them, that they are forgiven, and I would live in humble gratitude. But I don't. I mull over them and then try to make up excuses and turn them around and repent all over again. This cycle of self-condemnation and shame isn't from God. It finds its genesis in the Accuser, as he subtly yet relentlessly reminds me of them. But it's not his work alone. He's working in tandem with my proud heart, a heart that wants to be free of my consciousness of sin and need for a Savior.

There is a significant difference between conviction brought about by the Spirit and self-condemnation brought about by the Accuser as he acts on my pride. Conviction of sin draws me away from myself and toward God; it frees me to repent, grants me sorrow over offending my King, and floods me with relief in knowing that his smile still rests upon me. It eventuates in my loving Jesus more. Paul's words from Romans 8:1, "There is therefore now no condemnation for those who are in Christ Jesus," bestow great relief on my soul.

Self-condemnation, on the other hand, draws me down into myself and away from God. It makes me afraid and distrustful of him. It entraps me in unrelenting self-loathing and unbelief. It makes my heart cold toward the Lord; he's seen as a harsh taskmaster, a cruel tormenter. It makes me think of my Savior the way I should think of my enemy, and this reversal brings a vicious glee to the Accuser. Jesus slips from preeminence and is replaced by my shattered image of myself. Self-condemnation doesn't make me love Jesus more, because it's not essentially about him. It's about me.

In Revelation 12, John tells us how to overcome these attacks from our Accuser. He writes, "They have conquered him by the blood of the Lamb and by the word of their testimony, for they loved not their lives even unto death" (Rev. 12:11).

How do we conquer our enemy and his damning accusations? By working hard at being good? By rehearsing our good works to ourselves? No. Of course not. There's only one way to conquer him, and it's by the blood of the Lamb who was slain expressly for all of our sin. "Oh yes," our testimony rings out as our Accuser seeks to flog us with our failures, "I do sin and sin grievously, but Jesus Christ was slain as a perfect lamb in my place. Thank you for reminding me of my sin because, although it grieves me, it also reminds me to love him more." Once you've warmed your heart to this truth, it's natural to break out into a gospel song of praise. You can smile now because you have thwarted Satan's attempts to draw you away from your loving Savior.

It's only this perspective on our sin that will propel us into radical, sold-out, zealous, holy, sacrificial living. If we're incessantly engrossed with ourselves and our failures, we won't have the faith or courage to lift one finger for the kingdom. We might work harder at adding onto our own kingdom and righteousness, but never his. On the other hand, if we're completely free from guilt and utterly assured of his forgiveness and love, then the appropriate response from our hearts will be more and more love for him demonstrated in an increasingly holy life.

Be careful not to get these steps out of order in your walk today: forgiveness and full assurance of your Savior's love and grace come first, *then* comes the pursuit of godliness. If you turn this around, you'll be playing right into your enemy's strengths. He wants you to focus on your merit or lack thereof instead of on the merit of Christ. He wants to entrap you in an endless cycle of pride and shame, which is why Paul encouraged the Corinthians to reaffirm their love for the erring brother who had repented of his sin. He wrote, "You should rather turn to forgive and comfort him, or he may be overwhelmed by excessive sorrow. So I beg you to reaffirm your love for him . . . so that we would not be outwitted by Satan; for we are not ignorant of his designs" (2 Cor. 2:7–8, 11).

What are Satan's designs? How can we be outwitted by him? We can play into his evil schemes by failing to remind ourselves and others about the soul-liberating power of the blood of the Lamb. Satan's design is to get you to remember your sin, *ad infinitum*, so that he can shut you away from Jesus Christ and his grace and mercy. You might pray:

Father,

Thank you that though you are continually aware of all the ways in which I dishonor you, you use even my sin to draw me closer to you. Thank you that you sent your precious Son as a lamb slain from the foundation of the world so that my soul would be completely free from condemnation. Thank you for silencing the accusations of my enemy and for the day when his wickedness will be silenced forever. Please keep me close to you at all times: when I sin and feel unworthy of you and when I obey and am tempted to dismiss my need for you.

AMEN

Day 7

Unfazed by Grace?

The servant fell on his knees, imploring him,
"Have patience with me, and I will pay you everything."

MATTHEW 18:26

H ere we are, at the end of our first week together. I trust that your
soul has been warmed and liberated by the few days we've spent
finding comfort in his grace. Today we are going to consider how
grace impacts not only our self-perception but also how we perceive
and treat others.

If you recall, I've been saying that a life of godliness is impossible
without an awareness of lavish grace. Today I will tell you why, but
before I do, here are a few questions to direct your thinking:

- How quick are you to forgive others?
- How often do you rehearse others' sins?
- Do you ever hold a grudge?
- Are you doing so now?
- If I said the name of *that* one person, would you instantly fly off the
  handle and want to repeat everything she's done against you?

If you answered in the affirmative to any of these questions, what
follows will help you understand the parallels between your grasp of
grace and your graciousness toward others.

Jesus tells us of a servant who owed his king an immense amount
of money. When it became apparent that the servant would be unable

to repay his debt, the king ordered him and his family sold for pay-ment. At this, the servant "fell on his knees, imploring him, 'Have patience with me, and I will pay you everything.' And out of pity for him, the master of that servant released him and forgave him the debt" (Matt. 18:26–27). Of course, you know how the story goes: later on, this servant found a fellow debtor and demanded repayment of a much smaller sum. But when this debtor begged for mercy, none was found. The servant ordered the debtor thrown into prison until all was repaid.

Whenever I hear this story I want that ungrateful wretch to be punished, don't you? But before we start demanding justice, let me ask you, what do you think was the unmerciful servant's primary problem? Yes, of course, he lacked mercy and gratitude. Although he had been shown mercy, he had none for his fellow debtor. In addition, he didn't have much gratitude for what he'd been given (remember, in essence his king had just given him a gift of ten thousand talents). Grateful? Hardly.

In order to understand his problem, let's look again at his response to the king: "Have patience with me, and I will pay you everything." This debtor thought that the way out of his trouble was by working hard. He thought that if the king would just be a little more patient, he'd be able to work off what he owed him. Jesus used hyperbole to make his point: the ungrateful debtor owed so much money he could never pay it back. Ten thousand talents? Not in a lifetime! But still, in pride, arrogance, and self-deceit, he thought his situation wasn't all that bad. He assumed that he could make amends if his master would give him more time to make it up to him. "Have patience!" was his cry. Then, in a stroke of mind-boggling generosity, the master forgave him all, but the debtor remained as he was: *convinced of his own innate goodness and ability to deliver himself.*

Maybe he secretly assumed that this gift was something he actu-ally deserved; maybe he smirked within himself, thinking how he had pulled the wool over his master's eyes. Or, maybe he really did believe that he was a responsible person who took care of his debts, worked hard, and paid his own way. (Can't you just hear his self-assured, proud thoughts?) In any event, it's obvious that he continued to believe in his own goodness. He had too high an opinion of himself and too low an opinion of the king. He was *unfazed by grace*. And so he went to a fellow servant and demanded what was rightfully his. "You owe me! Pay up or you'll be sorry!"

Now, let me ask you again: do you find it hard to forgive, especially that *one* person? Is there someone who owes you? Whether that person has made your life difficult and owes you an apology or impugned your character and damaged your reputation, do you think he's in your debt? What if he's never asked you for mercy or promised to repay? What if he continues to harm you? Is your heart so filled with gratitude and mercy that you're overflowing with it *for him*? Or, to put it another way, are you, too, unfazed by grace?

Do you see our dilemma? We're each one of us that ungrateful wretch Jesus spoke of, and we all condemn him as though we weren't. We are the ones who cry, "Unfair! Foul!" at this story and yet shun those who fail to treat us with love and respect. We're the ones who judge those who crucified our King, and yet it was for our very sins that he walked up Golgotha's steep path. And yet, and yet . . . Jesus continues to love. Can you love like that? No, of course not.

This is where "proclaiming his death" is so important for your soul. I imagine that you might feel pretty guilty right now, but that's the wrong response. This understanding of your inability to love your neighbor isn't primarily meant to make you focus on yourself and your unwillingness to forgive; it's meant to drive you to Jesus. It's meant to strip you of your self-assurance and belief in your ability to reform yourself. It's meant to make you thankful that he loved his neighbor perfectly in your place and that that record of love is now yours. The only way you can begin to love those you hate is to drench—and I mean absolutely drench—your proud, despairing, demanding soul in these words: "Jesus died for sinners."

He has great pity for you and has released you and forgiven you of the great debt that you owed him. And although you'll continue to fail to love your neighbor, he never will. Now, because of the stubborn grace that loves you in your selfishness, you can be at liberty to love others. You might pray:

Father,

I have been forgiven so much, and yet I continue to harbor ill will, anger, and bitterness. Instead of loving my neighbor, I hate him; and yet, I'm just like him. Lord, thank you that you haven't given me what I deserved. In your lavish generosity, you humbled yourself and became just like me so that you could love and die in my place. Thank you that you continue to pour out your grace on me. Cause me to drink freely of this grace and believe that you love me like this. Thank you also for reminding me that I can never repay what I owe and that the proper response is simply to say, "Thank you." Thank you, Jesus.

AMEN

Day 8

Jesus, Remember Me

And he said,
"Jesus, remember me when you come into your kingdom."

LUKE 23:42

Since the beginning of time, there have only been three kinds of people. Yes, there are young and old, Asian, European, Indian, and African, famous and obscure, the privileged and the poor, educated and untaught, beautiful and plain, but only three nevertheless. And, in fact, we can easily observe all three in just one place, stripped and depicted in death, hung on a cross outside Jerusalem two thousand years ago.

After yesterday's challenge, I want to reemphasize the truth about who we are and what we need. Ultimately, our primary need is not trying harder to love the unlovely. Endless self-effort and its resultant guilt *never* generate love for those who mistreat us. Motivation to love and forgive our debtors is found only while resting in the love and forgiveness of our Savior. "Be kind to one another, tenderhearted, forgiving one another, *as God in Christ forgave you*" (Eph. 4:32). The only hope we have of being kind, tenderhearted, and forgiving is to remember how God in Christ has already forgiven us.

Now we're ready to find ourselves in the company of the three men who represent all mankind. Here's the narrative from Luke's Gospel where we're witness to the dreadful out working of Rome's cruel justice system:

> Two others, who were criminals, were led away to be put to death
> with him. And when they came to the place that is called The Skull,
> there they crucified him, and the criminals, one on his right and
> one on his left. . . . One of the criminals who were hanged railed at
> him, saying, "Are you not the Christ? Save yourself and us!" But
> the other rebuked him, saying, "Do you not fear God, since you are
> under the same sentence of condemnation? And we indeed justly, for
> we are receiving the due reward of our deeds; but this man has done
> nothing wrong." And he said, "Jesus, remember me when you come
> into your kingdom." And he said to him, "Truly, I say to you, today
> you will be with me in Paradise." (Luke 23:32–33, 39–43)

Here we find three men in what appear to be like circumstances.
Each has been judged guilty of a capital crime; the sentence has been
carried out, the bodies have been stripped and beaten; their souls
have been humiliated and terrified; spikes have been driven into six
wrists and ankles; crossbeams have been hoisted up, and nothing but
an inevitable, protracted, excruciating road to death awaits. But look
closer.

There are two men here who are criminals. Neither of these
criminals can save himself; they are both utterly helpless. Their hands
and feet nailed to a cross, they can't make amends or restitution, and
no one is interested in their story. They can't even breathe without
great pain, and with every breath the desire for oblivion grows. All
they are capable of doing is suffering and dying.

This is an exact representation of the spiritual condition of everyone who has ever lived. We are, each of us, guilty criminals completely
unable to save ourselves. There was no escape from crucifixion. There
should have been no escape for us. We are all guilty, weak, and helpless, shackled to our sin and inability to change with no prospect in
sight except that of endless suffering and ultimate death.

One of the criminals is angry and rails at Jesus. "If you are who
you say you are, then do something! Save yourself and us!" The other
is humble and contrite. "Jesus, remember me." See how both criminals are the same: both are completely powerless; both have been
judged by the law and found worthy of death. Neither has any hope
for escape. What is the difference between the two? Both ask to be
saved, but one does so in faith and the other in unbelief and anger.

Perhaps the scoffing man had learned that he could manipulate people with anger or sarcasm. He continues to trust in himself, and if he can't obtain his freedom, he's going to go down fighting. The other man knows what he deserves: "We are receiving the due reward of our deeds." In one sense this condemned criminal is absolutely right. He transgressed Roman law, and he was dying for it. But in another sense he was absolutely wrong, for he was about to receive the due reward for someone else's deeds. He pleads for mercy, "Jesus, remember me."

What does Jesus want from us? What can we offer him? He has no illusions; he doesn't sentimentally wish we were a bit nicer. "He knows our frame; he remembers that we are dust" (Ps. 103:14). Even when we dress ourselves up in our Sunday best and sing, "Praise the Lord," he knows the truth. He knows better than we do that we are utterly unable to reform ourselves. He knows that we are lost, shackled criminals who have no hope for real change without his saving intervention.

Now, my question to you is this: Do you see yourself in this way? Have you utterly despaired of offering anything to him that will make you worthy of his love? Do you know that kind of liberty? What did the repentant thief have to offer? Nothing. And yet, the Father had chosen him from before the foundation of the world. He had arranged that he suffer crucifixion on this particular day so that he would have this brief conversation with his Son. The Father anticipated†welcoming him into his kingdom. He had decreed, "This is my child." So he gave him the grace of self-knowledge and the courage to say, "Remember me."

What can we say? Simply this: "Nothing in my hands I bring." Why? Because, like these criminals, our hands remain shackled by sin and weakness. We are utterly incapable of producing any good that would pass the test of God's scrutiny. So all we can do is plead, "Jesus, remember me." And when we do, what is the Lord's response? "Today you will be with me in Paradise." He doesn't say, "Tsk-tsk, be assured that I remember you, and just as soon as you start loving that fellow who irritates you or stop gossiping about that girl, I'll let you have a peek in at my Paradise." No, that's not what he says. He knows what we are better than we do, and still he says, "You will be with me in Paradise." He took on everything that it means to be a condemned human. He hung on the cross with us. He took on everything that needed to be taken on so that we could be with him. He prays, "Father, forgive them."

The two powerless, ruined criminals hanging on The Skull are you and me, although one is angered and damned, the other humble and saved. But there is a third Man there who captures our attention, and his presence transforms everything. In one way he's different from the other two men; in another way he's made himself just like them. He represents us, too, but he is unique in all history. He was the only innocent. He was the perfect law keeper. He is God. Of the three, he was the only one who had the power to deliver himself, but because he wanted to open Paradise to you and me, he didn't move. He stayed where he was, "numbered with the transgressors" (Isa. 53:12; see also Luke 22:37), numbered with us because he loves us.

So today, when you're tempted to be unloving, don't focus solely on your failure; don't rage or despair or hide from him. Instead pray, "Jesus, remember me. Illumine my eyes to your love and to the Paradise that awaits, and help me now to love because you are loving me. Amen." Is it really that simple? Yes, it is that simple, that humble. What more could a shackled criminal do?

Day 9

Consider Him

Consider him who endured from sinners such hostility against himself, so that you may not grow weary or fainthearted.

HEBREWS 12:3

Over the twenty-plus years I've been counseling, there's one thing that I can almost always count on happening in the counseling room: people want to get over it (whatever *it* is) and they want to get over it right away. Whether *it* is a problem in their marriage or some troubling personal sin, they're usually ready to make any short-term sacrifice. They know they are going to have to work at it, but they expect immediate results, and the thought of having to struggle against a thorny or habitual sin over the long haul doesn't quite fit into their scheme of things. I'll admit that I'm the same. The long, hard struggle with sin is not something I enjoy any better than anyone else. I, too, want to get over *it*, and I want to get over it now.

The writer of Hebrews offers a different perspective, though. He writes:

> Let us . . . lay aside every weight, and sin which clings so closely, and let us run with endurance the race that is set before us, looking to Jesus, the founder and perfecter of our faith, who for the joy that was set before him endured the cross, despising the shame, and is seated at the right hand of the throne of God. Consider him who endured from sinners such hostility against himself, so that you may not grow weary or fainthearted. (Heb. 12:1–3)

From this passage we learn that our struggle against sin isn't something we're going to be able to hurry through, no matter how determined we may be. Our sins are weights; they cling closely to us. We learn that our slow change into Christlikeness is not a sprint but an endurance race. And because it's a marathon instead of a 100-yard dash, we're all tempted to grow weary and faint-hearted.

I want you to notice how many times the word *endurance* or *endure* is used in this passage. In the original language, all three times it has the connotation of patience, submitting to trial or waiting underneath something difficult. This passage encourages us to continue to persevere even though it seems as if we're not making any headway, or that we'll just never get it right.

Sometimes we find an analogy of gospel-truth in fiction that can be very helpful. J. R. R. Tolkien's *Lord of the Rings* illustrates this struggle against indwelling sin almost perfectly. Frodo's trip from the Shire to Mount Doom to destroy the Ring of Power gets us close to understanding the marathon we've been called to run. Frodo's journey was no walk in the park. And even when, after facing innumerable dangers, he finally arrived at the precipice of the mountain, he resisted, just as he was poised to annihilate the ring.

That's it. That's the nature of sin. We love it and we hate it. We know it's killing us yet still we pet it and want it near. Of course, this analogy breaks down because our problem isn't a ring hanging on a chain around our necks. No, this dreadful wickedness lives within us, in our own hearts, and it isn't willing to surrender without a battle. Would that we could, in one great act of will, hurl it away from us to be forever free!

If our expectation is that we should be able to take four simple steps to succeed in our struggle against sin, Hebrews warns that we'll despair and be self-condemning when we continue to fail. We'll become despondent and exhausted. This is one of the reasons why people run from seminar to seminar, why they pile up self-help books, and why they spend millions of dollars every year for psychotherapy.

Our problem is that we don't see the depth or power of our sin or how we're to continually fight against it.

So just how powerful is this sin that "clings so closely"? In the original language of the Bible, sin is likened to "a competitor who thwarts a racer in every direction."[1] Sin has an advantage because it's not in a hurry. It can wait, and whenever you make a move in any direction, it will seek to block you. No mere human has ever been able to conquer its power on his own.

I've painted a pretty bleak picture, haven't I? If this battle is so difficult, why don't we just give up? That would seem reasonable if it weren't for the gospel. The gospel teaches us that instead of focusing on ourselves and our closely clinging sin, we've got to focus on, to consider, Jesus. We've got to look away from our sin, whether because it's alluring and drawing us toward it or because it's condemning and pushing us into ourselves and away from our Savior. We must patiently focus all our attention on him. We've got to think on, ponder, or consider, Jesus. Every aspect of the gospel is meant to encourage us in our war against sin. Of course, we should be aware enough of our sin that we seek to repent of it and are grateful for the cross, but that's not where our thoughts should settle.

Our thoughts should be steadfastly riveted on what Jesus has done. He began our faith (or we wouldn't have it), and he's committed to bring it all the way to completion. We will have victory; there will be a day when sin and all its sorrows will be wiped away. Christ's ultimate victory over our sin and weakness is assured because he's seated at the right hand of his Father. The joy that he anticipated as he faced the cross, thinking nothing of its shame, was simply the joy of bringing millions of redeemed men and women— you and I—into his family. He endured hostility from the very people he had been sent to redeem so that we would know the joy of sharing his defeat of sin.

---

[1] *Euperistatos* (yoo-per-is'-tat-os). Biblesoft's *New Exhaustive Strong's Numbers and Concordance with Expanded Greek–Hebrew Dictionary*. © 1994, 2003 Biblesoft, Inc. and International Bible Translators, Inc.

Father,

Please help me know my sin so that I might repent of it, but then cause me to see your Son. I pray that no sin, no idol, no failure would capture my view, but Jesus alone. Cause me to see his faithfulness as he persevered through countless sorrows. Make his life loom large in my estimation so that I might draw from it the nourishment I need to persevere with faithfulness in running this race. I trust that you will sustain me and make me completely victorious when it pleases you to do so, and in the meantime, please grant me patience, faith, and strength to continue to war.

AMEN

Day 10

Not Good Enough

*I do not nullify the grace of God, for if righteousness
were through the law, then Christ died for no purpose.*

GALATIANS 2:21

I'm sure that you remember the story of Moses and the receiving of
the Law at Mount Sinai. God had delivered the children of Israel
from miserable slavery in Egypt with great power and compassion
and brought them to himself. When they came to Mount Sinai, Moses
relayed the Lord's words to them:

> You yourselves have seen what I did to the Egyptians, and how I
> bore you on eagles' wings and brought you to myself. Now there-
> fore, if you will indeed obey my voice and keep my covenant, you
> shall be my treasured possession among all peoples, for all the earth
> is mine; and you shall be to me a kingdom of priests and a holy
> nation. (Ex. 19:4–6)

In his desire to bless and have communion with his creation, the
Lord declared his intention to have a people for himself, a "treasured
possession," a "kingdom of priests, a holy nation." The qualification
for inclusion in this special covenant people was simply this: "Obey
my voice and keep my covenant." When the Israelites heard these
words, they joyously responded, "All that the LORD has spoken we
will do" (Ex. 19:8).

Even though Israel had good intentions, their history speaks something less than immediate and grateful obedience. After a second time of rehearsing covenant requirements and the people agreeing to it, Moses went up onto the mountain for forty days and nights to be with the Lord and receive the Law from him. While he was delayed in the presence of God, the Israelites became impatient and made a god for themselves to "go before them" (Ex. 32:1).

I can imagine that, from their perspective, they thought they were helping the Lord. They knew they needed a god to protect them from their enemies and bless them as they traveled to the Promised Land. They didn't think they were defecting from the Lord; indeed, at the same time that they "rose up to play" they offered burnt offerings and peace offerings to the Lord. In their sinful reasoning, they believed that they needed something more than the Lord. They wanted him, but they wanted their idols too.

It didn't take them long to pervert themselves and renege on everything they had promised to do. "All that the LORD has spoken we will do" quickly became "and the people sat down to eat and drink and rose up to play" (Ex. 32:6). But the rebellion didn't stop with the people, did it? On numerous occasions Aaron himself fell. And then later, even Moses, the meekest man who ever lived (Num. 12:3) failed. In self-reliance, anger, and unbelief, he struck the rock (Num. 20:10–12). *Not even Moses, the giver of the law, was able to keep the law.*

If Moses, such a meek and faithful believer, was unable to enter the land he so earnestly desired to see because of his anger, disobedience, and unbelief, is it reasonable to assume that we'll be able to enter into God's covenant blessings by our works?

Here's another one of those occasions when Paul makes statements that are meant to astonish us. He writes:

> We know that a person is not justified by works of the law but through faith in Jesus Christ, so we also have believed in Christ Jesus, in order to be justified by faith in Christ and not by works of the law, because by works of the law no one will be justified. . . . I do not nullify the grace of God, for if righteousness were through the law, then Christ died for no purpose." (Gal. 2:16, 21)

The Lord's covenant offer to the nation of Israel was clear: obey my law and you will be a treasured possession to me. But no mere human has been able to do so, not even a man of sterling character like Moses, a man who saw the Lord face-to-face and received the Law directly from his hand. Here's the bald truth: you and I are so completely unable to obey the law that we can't do so even when we want to. We may have good intentions, but the ability to fulfill those intentions is not present within us.

"Yes, yes," you might be agreeing, "that was true before I came to Christ. But now that I'm justified, I've got to work hard." Yes, it's true that we are called to zealously work and seek to obey. We've been given the power of the Spirit and a new nature. Yes, the ultimate power of sin in our lives has been broken. But what we have to remember here is that Paul isn't writing to unbelievers, telling them how to get saved. He's writing to the Galatian church, to believers who had succumbed to the heresy that obedience to the law had to be added to their faith in Christ. They had been deceived into thinking that they needed a bit of faith in themselves, too. They didn't think they were deserting the Lord; they were just adding to their faith a touch of law keeping, a little proud (and damning) self-righteousness.

Paul's response to that way of thinking is so adamant, it's like he's shouting at them. Do you believe that you'll be his "treasured possession" only if you obey? You're nullifying the grace of God! Do you believe that your continued inclusion in his "holy nation" is based on your righteousness? If so, then "Christ died for no purpose." Why? Because "by works of the law no one [including you and me] will be justified."

So then, God's intention to have a people who are his treasured possession is not thwarted one whit by your works (or lack of them). You see, he's gotten his "chosen race," his "royal priesthood," a "holy nation, *a people for his own possession*" (1 Pet. 2:9) by *his Son's* work. He pours out mercy on people who couldn't earn mercy. Our response is to continually, joyfully, loudly proclaim "the excellencies of him who called you out of darkness into his marvelous light." Rejoice with me:

My Dear Father,

Thank you for your mercy. Thank you that you've done for me what I never could have done for myself. You've sovereignly made me your treasured possession because you've granted to me the righteous record of your Son. Forgive me when I become impatient with my growth in holiness, rely on myself or my own good intentions, and seek to nullify grace. Keep me from trusting in myself and make me love you today, I pray.

AMEN

Day 11

Perfected for All Time

*For by a single offering he has perfected for all time
those who are being sanctified.*

HEBREWS 10:14

I have to admit that it's pretty difficult for me to read words such as "perfected for all time" and have faith to apply them to myself. It might be different if the passage read, "perfected for a few moments when meditating on the cross," or "pretty okay for a while." But "perfected for all time"? Hardly. All I have to do is think of the way that I failed to love a screeching child this morning or longed for a pain-free life filled with peace and ease this afternoon, and I can see that there's a great divide between "perfected for all time" and my daily life. Is it the same for you? Let's take a moment to look more deeply into this passage to encourage our faith as we face our oh-so-less-than-perfect performances today.

The book of Hebrews was written primarily to, well, the Hebrews, people who were familiar with the demands, ceremonies, and sacrifices of the Jewish temple system. In that system offerings and sacrifices had to be made over and over again, since the blood of mere animals, although commanded by the Lord, could only cover sin, never remove it. The blood of bulls and goats could not atone for the sin that permeated the heart of the human lawbreaker.

In the Judaism of the first century, people were well aware of their problem with sin, probably more so than we are today. Today many of us think we have "issues" caused by unloving parents, hyperactive children, persistent singleness, or inconsiderate spouses. Even as Christians we are generally not as aware of God's unchanging and relentless demand for perfection as these early Jews were. They knew very well that they were culpable for their failure to obey, and they knew the sentence for failure: curses and death. Their imperfection was persistent and willful. But it was to these people that this passage first spoke.

You have got to get an idea of the shock the early believers would have felt upon reading these words. Perfected for all time? How could those words be uttered about anyone? They knew full well the sacrifices required to atone for their sin: a young bird, a goat, a bull, a spotless lamb. They were well aware that their sins weren't some minor blemish but were serious enough that a living creature had to suffer and die. This wasn't merely a philosophical or theological persuasion. For their unbelief, warm blood streamed onto sticky stone; because of their covetousness, animals cried out in terror. And for those who lived in Jerusalem, there was the smoke that hung continually over the temple mount. Listen to hear the bleating of the soon-silenced lamb; smell the acrid stench of burning hair and flesh; see the white robes of the high priest darkly stained. They knew their imperfections—they were lawbreakers.

In the midst of all this, all they could do was hope their efforts were enough to atone for what they'd done, even though they knew it really wasn't enough; the deathly sacrifice would just have to be repeated again and again. Into that bloody, earthy, repetitive system of religion and death came these words:

> And every priest stands daily at his service, offering repeatedly the same sacrifices, which can never take away sins. But when Christ had offered for all time a single sacrifice for sins, he sat down at the right hand of God. . . . For by a single offering *he has perfected for all time* those who are being sanctified. (Heb. 10:11–12, 14)

The early Jewish Christians experienced something that their predecessors had never known: complete freedom from guilt, rest from the law's cruel lash, infinite acceptance before a holy God. Think of their joy and relief. No wonder they turned the world upside down.

Jesus Christ, the ultimate high priest, had accomplished what no other high priest had ever even dared to attempt. On the cross he spilled *the blood of God to appease the wrath of God*. This blood was so precious, being the very blood of the infinite, incarnate God, that just this one sacrifice was completely sufficient to atone for and bring to perfection all who would believe in it. Just one sacrifice was necessary to perfect them, to perfect you.

Very few, if any, of us have ever tried to atone for our sins by shedding the blood of an animal. We view that system of sacrifice as unthinkable, archaic. But that doesn't mean that we don't try to atone for our sins in other ways. When we see that we've failed again we make resolutions.

"I'll do better tomorrow."

"I'll make it up by praying more tonight or by being nice to that nasty coworker."

"I'll sacrifice something I want to do to prove that I'm really serious about doing better. I'll not let myself enjoy the blessings of the day because I know that I don't deserve them."

Just like the early readers of this letter, we need a deep draught of this truth: Jesus Christ offered one sacrifice for sin and in doing so he absolutely perfected those who are (still) being changed or sanctified. Our ongoing struggle against sin isn't proof that his blood was ineffective or that something more needs to be done. No, the Spirit assures us that we're absolutely perfected right now. He made one offering for sin and then sat down by his Father's side, watching over our journey toward maturity.

Our high priest's spotless garment was soiled with the filth of our sin and then the precious blood of the eternal God flowed down over it, cleansing it away *forever*. When we spend our days in an endless pursuit of self-improvement, trying over and over again to "get our act together," or trying to excuse our sin because, after all, "nobody's perfect," we are, in essence, devaluing the blood of Jesus Christ, the perfect man who is also God.

My Father,

What you have done for me is nearly beyond belief! You have made me—a hopeless, rebellious, unbelieving sinner—absolutely and eternally perfect.

By your sacrifice you've assured me that any sacrifice for sin that needed to be made has been made, and all I have to do is believe that your blood really is that valuable. Thank you for forgiving me especially when I dishonor you by thinking that my meager, miserable, pride-driven sacrifices would somehow appease your great wrath at sin. You've made me perfect, and you're perfecting me. Thank you, Lord. I believe.

AMEN

Day 12

Motivated by Love

"If you love me, you will keep my commandments."

JOHN 14:15

Imagine this scene: it's 5:47 PM; the savory aroma of the roast fills your home and the table is carefully set. You diligently finish up the final preparations for company, and then you walk by your children's bathroom. To your great dismay, there, in several piles on the floor, you see yesterday's clothing, underwear and all. The mirror is spotted with water, dried dribbles of toothpaste remain where your darlings carelessly spit them this morning, and there's no toilet paper in the holder. You clearly remember telling them to take care of this mess earlier, so you go in search of them. What are they doing? Playing, of course. Get the picture? Of course you do.

Now, how will you motivate your children to obey you and get that bathroom cleaned up? Is it possible that your words might sound something like this: "You know, if you really loved Mommy, you'd obey me when I ask for your help. You can say that you love me all you want, but you need to prove it to me by your actions. Come on, kids, don't you love your poor mother? Please do what I've asked." Yes, I can hear it now. Guilt—the gift that keeps on giving.

It is true that the object of our love can *always* be detected in our behavior. If these errant children love their mother, they will seek to help her. In like manner, our lifestyle does prove the sincerity of our claim of love for God. *If love for God isn't present in our heart, then*

Godward obedience will be absent in our life. Jesus recognized the indissoluble connection between love and obedience. In the passage above he is teaching us about obedience, but not the way we teach our children. He isn't piling on the guilt or hoping we'll feel sorry for him and clean up our act. No, instead he knows that love for him is the only incentive that will stand up during trial and temptation, so he teaches us this vital relationship between love and obedience.

Jesus is lovingly stating a fact, but he's also making a precious promise: love *will* motivate behavior. He completely knows us, even the inmost thoughts of our hearts. He knows of our desire to obey and our shame and sadness because of our failures. But he also knows this: as our love for him grows, our obedience will grow, too.

Let me explain how the truth that love motivates obedience usually plays out in my heart. I think, *Okay, I've got the "love God" part down, so now I need to concentrate on being more and more obedient to prove it.* It's right there that I fail to get the emphasis right. I gloss over the motivating role that love plays and focus in on what I need to *do* instead. I mistakenly assume that my love for him is what it should be. But this verse isn't primarily meant as a correction to lazy believers. It is meant to tell us what the *key to obedience* is.

The key to a godly life is not more and more self-generated effort. Instead, Jesus is saying, "Love me and your obedience will flow naturally from that love." The secret to obedience isn't formulaic steps found in a self-help book. It is a relentless pursuit of love for him. How then do I cultivate the sincerity of love that motivates obedience? By focusing more intently on his love for me than on my love for him, more on his obedience than mine, more on his faithfulness than mine, more on his strengths than mine.

The apostle John knew that the only way love for God could be created in us was through a grasp of God's prior love to us. He simply stated, "We love because he first loved us" (1 John 4:19). The plain truth is that my love for God (and hence, my obedience) will grow as I cultivate my comprehension of his vast love for me. This is the wonderful promise of our Savior and the only sure method for true growth in godliness.

If we neglect this key by focusing too narrowly on ourselves, our success or failure, then we'll become mired down in guilt or pride, neither of which will stimulate loving obedience. If, on the other hand, we intently focus on how we've been loved, irrevocably, eternally, freely, and without merit, if we contemplate how our obedience (or lack of it) doesn't faze his love one whit, then we'll find within our hearts a growing desire to obey. Why? Because *love like that changes people*. It draws us toward him; it makes us want to be like him; it makes obedience attractive. Resting in the awareness of our perfect acceptance before him and in his intense desire to have us for his own will cause us to want to please him. It will make us love him, and love for him will always eventuate in godliness.

Does this key to obedience guarantee that we'll never struggle with sin? No. We'll continue to struggle because our love will remain imperfect. It is weak and wavering because we can't see him as he is. We're seeing only a dim reflection of Jesus' beauty through the polluted window of our sin-stained souls, so we're not transformed into loving beings—yet (1 Cor. 13:8–12).

We're still vulnerable to Satan's lies. We can be deceived into thinking that our Savior is cruel, unfaithful, unloving, foolish. His beauty is distorted by our sin-skewed myopia, so we leave him and chase after what sparkles before us. Other gods whisper promises of love and happiness. We disobey. But our Redeemer doesn't leave us there. He patiently and gently draws us back into his loving arms and reassures us of his overwhelming compassion, mercy, and grace.

Your Savior isn't like your mother. He isn't trying to motivate you through guilt or pity. His love is fervent, eternal, uncompromising. Rest there, drink there, luxuriate in the warm sunshine of his smile; grow strong in his everlasting embrace. Confront your own sinfulness, yes, but only after you've remembered his love for you. Then love him and obey.

Day 13

The Joy of Obedience

For this is the love of God, that we keep his commandments.
And his commandments are not burdensome.

1 JOHN 5:3

In yesterday's reading I wrote that a fervent love for God makes "obedience attractive." Have you ever thought, *If I would just treat my spouse* (or parent, employer, children, or neighbor) *the way the Lord commands, I know I would be happier, the relationship I have with him would be blessed, and the Lord would be pleased?* When I think about obedience in that way, it's attractive to me, too.

Although I easily imagine the joys of obedience, I'll admit that obedience is not as easily adopted. I, too, have thought that a life of loving obedience would be delightful, that is, until I'm confronted with the choice of giving up something that, at that moment, I love more. Then the cost of obedience just seems crushingly laborious. So I hedge and I fudge and I think of reasons why "just this once" I shouldn't obey. At these times I don't think obedience is attractive. It seems like a heavy burden.

This passage in 1 John has mystified me: "This is the love of God, that we keep his commandments. And his commandments are not burdensome" (1 John 5:3). Frankly, I've wondered why John wrote that God's commandments were "not burdensome." During times of trial, when faced with a difficult obedience, "burdensome" is definitely the language I would choose to describe my struggle. In fact, when it comes right down to it, sometimes it feels like obedience is just too much to ask. The cost is too high, my love for him too weak.

Even so, the theme that love motivates joyous and obedient service is found frequently in Scripture. The story of Jacob and Rachel illustrates it well. You'll recall that Jacob indentured himself as a servant to his uncle, Laban, in order to win Rachel, Laban's daughter, for a wife. Why? Because Jacob loved her. And so he worked day in and day out for seven years to earn the right to have her as his wife. Lest we think that this service was easy, here's how Jacob described it later: "By day the heat consumed me, and the cold by night, and my sleep fled from my eyes" (Gen. 31:40). And yet Jacob remembered his service as years that "seemed to him but a few days because of the love he had for her" (Gen. 29:20). Think of that! Seven hard years flew by like just a few days. Love was the reason. The years of work he endured were not burdensome. They were years of work, yes, but not burdensome work.

Jesus told a story of people who had an opposite perspective. In this parable a landowner hired day laborers for his vineyard at an agreed-upon wage. During the day he brought in others to work, and then at the end of the day he doled out their earnings. Those who labored all day and those who labored only for one hour both received an equal wage, what they had contracted for. "These last worked only one hour," the angry workers complained, "and you have made them equal to us who have borne the burden of the day and the scorching heat" (Matt. 20:12).

Although these disgruntled workers received what was rightfully theirs, they were dissatisfied. They had no filial relationship to this landowner; they were day laborers, not sons. They had no concern for the other workers, either. They were individuals, not family members. What was work like for them? They complained that they had "borne the burden of . . . the scorching heat." Did the hours fly by because they were glad to serve their master? No, absolutely not. Their labor was grinding; they struggled until that scorching sun finally set so they could get what they had earned and leave. Their labor was burdensome.

In another familiar parable, that of the prodigal son and his brother, we find the eldest son irate because his father had warmly welcomed his brother home. Notice how he described his obedience: "Look, these *many years* I have served you" (Luke 15:29). Obedience was onerous to him because love was lacking. He saw his father as nothing more than a demanding taskmaster, so he was resentful of his father's generosity, mercy, and love. He meticulously tallied up his every hour and act of obedience. Life in this household was only a burden to be borne.

It's easy to see the difference between Jacob and those who were only working for their wages. Jacob's work flowed out of a heart of love. The other workers were in it only for themselves: they had obligations, life was hard, they were just trying to survive another day. There's ease and joy in love-driven obedience, miserliness and drudgery in duty-driven obedience.

Your Savior's love-driven obedience was envisaged in Psalm 40:8: "I delight to do your will, O my God." Like Jacob before him, Jesus' work to obtain his bride was a "delight" to him because of the great love he had for her. The One who created the sun languished under its scorching beams and struggled to keep warm when the cold penetrated his cloak at night. The One who multiplied loaves was hungry; he who sustained the universe by his word was tired. He perfectly completed the years of work his Father had given him to do, and his reward was given to others who joined in at the last moment. His inheritance was bestowed upon those who gleefully deserted him and spent their days in riotous living. The payment he earned was granted to proud self-righteous ones who disdained him. But he called it all his *delight* because he loved. He gladly laid down his life for his bride.

I'm sure that now, from the perspective of heaven, the days he spent on earth seem but a moment to him because of his love for you. And these difficult years that you're apart from him will seem like nothing more than "one night spent in an inconvenient motel" when your eyes finally rest upon his face.

Is obedience a burden or a delight? Is loving your neighbor, whoever that may be, a source of joy or a grinding drudgery? As you consider the answer to these questions, please resist the temptation to be mired down in your failure to love. Instead, turn your heart toward him and thank him for the love he has for you.

Father,

Please reveal your love to me once again. Please cause me to love you and respond by delighting in doing your will. Holy Spirit, please renew my love for the Son and grant me the grace of loving obedience, for his glory I pray.

AMEN

Day 14

Glory to God Alone

"I am the LORD; that is my name;
my glory I give to no other,
nor my praise to carved idols."

ISAIAH 42:8

The Father's purpose in your life, indeed in all the world, is to glorify and magnify his Son (Col. 1:18). It is to make the One who seems insignificant and small to us as marvelous and precious as he really is. The Father's proclamation, "You are my beloved Son; with you I am well pleased" (Luke 3:22), will never cease to resound in heaven or on earth, and he wants us to hear these words and sing them out with all our hearts too.

How will the Father's loving desire to make much of his Son be accomplished? His goal to exalt his Son is accomplished when we delight in the fact that salvation is completely of the Lord, and not at all of us (Acts 4:10). Our inability to save ourselves and our utter dependence upon his grace and power exalt him rather than us. Just think: if we were able, by some Herculean effort, to obey the law and thereby ingratiate ourselves before the Lord, the glory, at least in part, would belong to us, wouldn't it? Our works, our determination, our wisdom, and our innate goodness would be magnified. And his incarnation, perfect life, sacrificial death, resurrection, and ascension would be diminished in our eyes. If we don't see ourselves as desperately lost and utterly helpless, Calvary will become a cosmic overreaction meant to save people who really aren't all that bad. Jesus Christ will be devalued; the beloved Son will not be loved or cherished as he should be.

Are you "well pleased" with him? Is he the "beloved Son" to you? We must see how desperately we needed and, yes, even today, continue to need him. We won't value or cherish him as we should until we openly and freely embrace our wretchedness and our utter inability to reform ourselves. Only then will we fall freely into his arms of grace and there joyfully exalt the salvation he has purchased with his blood. As we learn to despair of seeing any merit or power in our own goodness, we will see his merit and power for what it is: our only hope of salvation. This perspective, and only this perspective, will enable us to love him as he deserves to be loved.

Our utter inability to save ourselves or even to maintain our salvation once it's been granted to us brings great glory to the Son: it exalts his power, his purity, his grace, and his mercy. He didn't save people who had a case of spiritual sniffles. No, he saved the wretched, leprous, lame, blind, poor, captive, adulterous, murdering, vile scum of the earth (Luke 4:18–19). He saved the proud, moral, religious, and self-righteous too (once he demolished their self-trust so that they could see themselves for who they really were). He said that he came to seek and save the *lost* (Luke 19:10), the *soul-diseased*, and *unrighteous sinners* (Luke 5:31–32). He delights in saving all those who recognize their need, even those who boldly proclaim that they are the foremost offenders (1 Tim. 1:14–15).

He also saves those who come timorously, in shame, misunderstanding, and fear (Luke 8:44ff.). He comes to save those who know they need saving, because they are the only ones who will take what he has to offer: his spotless robe of righteousness for the polluted, self-aggrandizing, arrogant rags of their own good works. *His salvation is a great salvation, and he deserves to be greatly worshiped.*

Why do you suppose that there "will be more joy in heaven over one sinner who repents than over ninety-nine righteous persons who need no repentance" (Luke 15:7)? Is it because the angels are so happy for us? Yes, perhaps, in part, but only as it pertains to the honor of the Son. Every time one sinner repents, more praise and glory is brought to the Son. The King is being loved and glorified, and in that they rejoice. One more voice is being added to this enormous heavenly choir:

> After this I looked, and behold, a great multitude that no one could number, from every nation, from all tribes and peoples and languages, standing before the throne and before the Lamb, clothed in white robes, with palm branches in their hands, and crying out with a loud voice, "Salvation belongs to our God who sits on the throne, and to the Lamb!" (Rev. 7:9–12)

The truth about our twisted hearts, whether we're comfortable admitting it, is that we want very much to have a little bit of the glory come to us. We want to be able to approve of ourselves, to look at our record and say, "What a good girl am I!" Then when we fail, when we let ourselves or others down, we hide from God, give in to despair and self-indulgence or recommit to trying harder, over and over again in an endless cycle of self-righteousness, self-loathing, pride, and shame.

We are, as Paul Tripp teaches, "glory robbers." We want Christ's glory for ourselves. Jesus Christ is willing to share his righteousness with you, to impute to your record his perfect obedience. But his glory he will not share with anyone. You will not receive praise in heaven; no one will glorify your name. No one will say to you, "This person is here because of you." The praise will all belong to him because he has accomplished it all. Our desire to take his glory for our own isn't merely futile; it's an attack against his perfect work.

The humility that is the source of true worship must be born in you by the Spirit. On our own, we'll always cling to our good works, but the Holy Spirit was sent to help us to make much of him, and he delights in our doing so. As you consider this passage about Jesus from Isaiah 42, pray that the Spirit will illumine your eyes to your utter need for his grace and then fill your heart with songs of joy and praise:

Behold my servant, whom I uphold,
    my chosen, in whom my soul delights;
I have put my Spirit upon him;

. . . .

Thus says God, the LORD,
    who created the heavens and stretched them out,
    who spread out the earth and what comes from it,
who gives breath to the people on it
    and spirit to those who walk in it:

. . . .

I am the LORD; *that is my name;*
    my glory I give to no other.

. . . .

Sing to the LORD *a new song,*
    his praise from the end of the earth. . . .
Let them give glory to the LORD,
    and declare his praise in the coastlands. (vv. 1, 5, 8, 10, 12)

Day 15

From Suffering to Glory

Jesus said to her, "Did I not tell you that if you believed
you would see the glory of God?"

JOHN 11:40

During a conversation I had recently with a dear Christian friend,
she remarked, "I just don't understand why there has to be
so much suffering." From there she went on to describe numerous
long-standing trials in which several family members were wasting
away through disease and others were continually frustrated in what
seemed like godly pursuits.

I understood her confusion. If God loves us, and we believe that
he does, then why doesn't he use his power to prevent suffering? Why
do our children continue in rebellion? Why do we lose our parents
to the horrifying vacuity that is Alzheimer's? Why do godly Christian
couples try in vain to conceive while unbelievers abort their children?
Why do we suffer? Does our suffering mean anything to God, or is
he indifferent, detached, aloof?

We can learn much about the heart of God in our suffering by
looking in John 11 at the account of the death and resurrection of
Jesus' friend Lazarus. Here's how the narrative begins:

> Now a certain man was ill, Lazarus of Bethany, the village of Mary
> and her sister Martha. . . . So the sisters sent to him, saying, "Lord,
> he whom you love is ill." . . . Now Jesus loved Martha and her sister

and Lazarus. So, when he heard that Lazarus was ill, he stayed two days longer in the place where he was. (John 11:1, 3, 5–6)

What struck you as you read the passage above? Don't the statements, "Jesus loved" and "he stayed two days longer" seem incongruous to you? If I were writing this story, I would have said, "Jesus loved so he dropped everything and rushed to be with his friend and healed him." But that's not what we read, is it? It's obvious that Jesus' fierce love for his friends meant something different to him than it does to us. What made him wait?

Certainly, he could have hesitated out of self-protection or apathy. The religious leaders were scheming to kill him, so avoiding Jerusalem (and its suburbs) would have been understandable. But didn't he love his friend enough to risk their wrath? Besides, wasn't he able to heal from a distance? Was he simply apathetic, uncaring? From this side of the cross such questions seem blasphemous, but I'm sure they were the ones that plagued these women as they watched the life drain out of their beloved brother.

And so the hours dragged ever so slowly by while Mary and Martha waited at Lazarus's bedside. Whatever his ailment was, we can be sure of one thing: there was a depth of suffering and excruciating sorrow made all the worse by their friend's delay. How many times did they hear a greeting in the street and jump up, hoping to see their friend Jesus? How often did they try to encourage each other, "Don't worry, he'll come. He loves Lazarus." But as time passed, perhaps the sisters wondered if they had done something to offend. *Maybe he didn't really care that much after all. Perhaps he's just too busy; he wouldn't deliberately have deserted us, would he?*

Jesus waited twelve years to heal the woman with the issue of blood. Another lame man had been hoping for healing for thirty-eight years before Jesus commanded him, "Get up, take up your bed, and walk" (John 5:8). He waited four days to raise his friend from the dead. Why? Jesus tells us, "It is for the glory of God, so that the Son of God may be glorified through it" (John 11:4).

When we're facing the prospect of lifelong pain or the possibility of final separation from a beloved friend, it's easy to think that we know what would best glorify God. When it's my pain or loss, I think that God's glory would be seen most clearly in my immediate deliverance. But when I look at this story (and so many others), I see something different. I see Jesus raising a man who had been in the tomb four days, and I know that nothing is impossible. Sure, he could have instantly alleviated the family's suffering, but Jesus is more interested in our eternal cure than he is in our temporal relief.

Jesus is not a genie in a bottle nor is he a heartless despot. He is your compassionate Savior. That is why he waited until all hope was gone before he went back to Bethany, intent on blessing his friends and infuriating his enemies. He had already tallied up the cost of this act of love. He traversed the 25 miles to raise his friend from death and lay down his life.

He didn't delay because he was unfazed by his friends' sufferings. He was infuriated by the effects of sin (John 11:33, 38). He entered fully into their painful loss. The eternal Son of God, who celebrated in infinite bliss and glory, *wept* (John 11:35). And then he cried out in joyous power, "Lazarus, come out!" and in those three words he changed everything. Mary and Martha finally understood.

I don't know what you are suffering right now, but he does. He is not capricious, picking petals off a daisy: "I think I'll help them, I think I won't." He's bearing your suffering and has entered into every bit of it, but he is waiting. Perhaps your deliverance will come before you take your next breath; perhaps it will come as you take your last. I don't know. But I do know that he has made a promise to you: if you believe you will see the glory of God (John 11:40). Just imagine that. Hang on to him in faith and imagine that you will see the glory of God! Your eyes will be opened to see how truly wise, powerful, and good he is. Somehow, in some way hidden to your weak eyes, your suffering is making a way for that to happen. I don't know when your "Lazarus" will rise, but when he does, you will see something you never could have imagined. You will see God's glory, you will begin to see him as he is, and then you will understand.

My Father,

Please give me grace to believe. It's so easy for me to see what I'm suffering and to be confused about your glorious, mysterious purposes. Like my sisters Mary and Martha, I always want to say, "If you would just have been here . . . " It's easy for me to think that I can control you by my good works or that you don't really love me as I am. So I pray that in your grace you would remind me that you are here and that you're working toward a better good than I could ever imagine. You want me to see your glory, how wonderful and wise you are. Lord, help me believe that your glory is worth this suffering, just as you knew that my seeing it was worth yours.

AMEN

Day 16

See Him!

See what kind of love the Father has given to us, that we should be called children of God; and so we are. The reason why the world does not know us is that it did not know him.

1 JOHN 3:1

When Tom Hanks's character Forrest Gump humbly proclaimed, "I may be stupid, Jenny, but I know what love is," in a way he spoke for all of us. We all possess an innate awareness and understanding of love. From the youngest toddler who slobbers out, "Wub woo, Mama," to the family patriarch who labors ceaselessly so that his children will have it better than he did, our lives are tethered to love. Woven into every thread of our existence is the concept that love is the most important thing about who we are. When we are unloved, we feel that there must be something wrong with us; when we fail to love we know that we are blameworthy. "I should have loved him better" and "What's wrong with me, that I can't be loved?" are sentiments often heard in the counselor's office. How we're loved and how we love is, in many ways, the definition of who we are as humans.

The story of redemption is, in its purest form, a love story, but it's a love story unlike anything you could ever imagine. It's the story of God's love for you, but this love isn't just a sweet sentiment inscribed on a greeting card destined for next week's garbage bin. It's deeper and richer, and honestly a bit frightening. It's love that is willing to afflict itself and its beloved for a greater good.

In yesterday's reading I described it as "fierce." The story of your redemption is a story of fierce love. Because of his love, Jesus brought pain upon his friends, the little family in Bethany, and thereby brought pain upon himself. He wouldn't allow himself the luxury of loving them less than they needed to be loved. His love is not flimsy or self-serving; it's fierce. It's far more like Aslan's than Santa's.

Fierce love pours from the tip of the pen of John, the apostle of love. "See what kind of love the Father has given to us," he proclaims, "that we should be called children of God" (1 John 3:1). Likely you are familiar with the truth John points out here, but let me encourage you to push past detached facts, which can anesthetize the soul, to hear this breathtaking message. Picture him jumping up and down, waving his arms, seeking to awaken us from our stupor, while we muse, "Oh yes, God's love . . . la la la. . . . I'm his child. Isn't that nice," and then sink back into our comfy recliner, revisiting fantasies of how pleasant our lives would be if Santa really did visit us this year. "No, no! You're missing it!" he would be yelling. "This love is the most important thing about you; it changes and will change everything!"

Fierce love slips into Bethlehem, virtually unnoticed, as tears stream down the Virgin's face. It is heard in the baby's whimper as he's placed in the barren feeding trough. Then, at night, it secrets the family away, down to the isolation of despised Egypt, while a vicious despot slaughters toddlers. The glow of his fierce love grows on through the seemingly endless years of mundane family life in Nazareth. For a while the whispers about Mary die down, and then the Son explodes onto the scene.

"Isn't this Mary's son? You know, she was pregnant before they were married." "Who is this illegitimate nobody making himself out to be?" The embodiment of the Father's love overturns the commercial interests of the religious, commands hatred of one's own family, blesses children, and welcomes the demon-possessed.

His mother thinks with anguish, "Has he lost his mind?"

And then that fierce love poured every drop of an eternal hell's worth of wrath upon the bloodied head of its delight, and again he cries. "Father, why have you forsaken me?"

Shake off your boredom and apathy. God's love for you is fierce, self-afflicting, white-hot, life-transforming. The goal of this love is that you may be called God's daughter, God's son. All this pain and grief is bent in on one primary goal: your adoption and his eventual praise. Your relationship with the Creator of all there is has been secured in the blood and tears of love's delight. Your Father is no longer far off, no longer a stranger, no longer a judge. Now he's your Father. John wants us to see that we are called God's children because we *are* his children, even now.

But John rejoices that even though we're really and truly God's children now, "what we will be has not yet appeared" (1 John 3:2). A day will surely come when we'll be utterly transformed because the blinders of this temporal life will have been dissolved by light, and we'll finally see him as he really is. But today we stumble through the shadows, our eyes having grown accustomed to the darkness, our hearts comfortably ensnared by well-loved deceptions. "Wake up!" John is saying. "See his adopting love!" John directs our gaze to this love because only a fierce meditation on our adoption in Christ will breed the courageous zeal necessary in our war for purity. John writes, "Everyone who thus hopes in him purifies himself" (1 John 3:3).

So much of our lives as Christians is spent in futile doubt, weak questionings, and apathetic, self-serving strategies. In part, we fail in our war for purity because we spend too much time meditating on ourselves, our work, our growth. We have little hope for change because our hope is grounded in ourselves, in how we're doing, in whether God is proving his love by granting us every trifling desire or delivering us from heartbreaking trial. We've been deceived into believing that his love is passé, something we've already comprehended. It bores us. John's message, through the Spirit of the living Christ, calls to you today: "See!"

See him. See what your adoption cost him. See his commitment to his family, to you. Steep your soul in the warmth of his desire to have you for his own, and after you have done that, pursue the purity that is a mark of this fierce love.

Father,

I'll admit that your love both bores and frightens me. I mistakenly think that I understand it, so I skim over it as if it were yesterday's headlines.

But sometimes it breaks through and I begin to see what it's really like and I'm terrified, so I run from you. I numb my soul to its influences through futile amusements and self-assuring good deeds. I rarely start my day with the thought, "My Father, who art in heaven." Please forgive me for this and for neglecting what your adoption of me really means. I've taken this truth for granted and resisted your Fatherly intrusion into my life because I haven't trusted the goodness of your love. Please open my eyes and grant me grace to see you, your love, the security of my place in you, and the inevitability of my complete transformation, and then give me grace to draw near to you for strength to war against our enemies.

AMEN

Day 17

Freedom

*For freedom Christ has set us free; stand firm therefore, and
do not submit again to a yoke of slavery.*

GALATIANS 5:1

It wouldn't be an exaggeration to say that Paul was absolutely rabid
about our freedom in Christ. "For freedom Christ has set us free,"
he wrote, "stand firm therefore, and do not submit again to a yoke of
slavery" (Gal. 5:1). He knew firsthand what slavery to the law was
like; he had lived manacled to it his entire life. But now that he had
found true freedom in Christ it was the incessant theme of his every
thought.

Paul had deep fatherly affection for the Galatian church, but his
heart was tormented by reports about them. Somehow the Judaizers,
people who taught that their obedience to the law was necessary for
justification, had poisoned his dear children's faith. Although Paul
had warred so heroically to bring them to the liberty Christ had purchased for them, they had been ensnared again in a "yoke of slavery."
They had been fooled into believing that they had to add good works
to faith, that faith alone wasn't sufficient to make them acceptable
to God. So Paul shouted, "Watch out! Stand firm! Christ has set you
free so that you can live a free life. Never again let anyone bind the
fetters of the law upon you."

Paul was so infuriated at the false teachers that he said, "I wish
those who unsettle you would emasculate themselves!" (Gal. 5:12).

He didn't mince words. This freedom wasn't simply a preference for him; it was the very heart of the gospel. He had been a slave—to sin and the law—and now he was free.

Most of us realize that the Christian life is war. Our war against sin is a desperate blood-and-sweat conflict that will persist until we are perfected in glory. Although it's true that our Savior vanquished all sin on Calvary, we know that we still have to fight to maintain our freedom, because it's sin's nature to enslave and entangle our hearts in unbelief, idolatry, and self-love.

Yes, the Christian life is war, but it's not only a battle against slavery to sin. It's also a battle against slavery to law. There are two fronts in our war to maintain freedom: the obvious one against sin and the hidden one against works-righteousness. Most of us have missed that second war entirely, haven't we? Two wars? A war against slavery to good works?

In blinding us to the dangers of our "splendid vices" (Luther's phrase for works-righteousness), Satan has accomplished much. Of course, he would snicker if we lived debauched lives and never thought about obedience. But that tactic doesn't work on everyone, particularly not the religiously proud. So he tempts us to rely on the law to spruce things up a bit and assure us of God's approval. *I do believe that God loves me*, we muse, *but I'm sure he'd love me more if I went on the mission field or prayed longer or never yelled at my kids.* "This persuasion is not from him who calls you," Paul thunders. "A little leaven leavens the whole lump" (Gal. 5:8–9). Here's Paul's shocking message: just a smidgeon of works-righteousness, just a drop of minor law keeping (so that we're sure we're covering all our bases), will poison our entire soul.

Works-righteousness will enslave us, similar to more obvious sins, but it's far more dangerous because it appeals to our religious pride. It comes cloaked in something akin to genuine goodness. *I know that I don't have to get straight As, have people over every night, or wash my car every weekend, but I think it shows that I'm really serious about pleasing God and not like other people who take their salvation for granted.*

We smile conceitedly when we think that we're just a bit better than others. Satan is, of course, delighted to entrap us in either debauchery or pride; he doesn't care which. But religious pride so perfectly works to dishonor Christ. Satan gloats over legalistic religiosity because it always results in hypocrisy. Pride will keep people out of Christ's kingdom just as easily as the lower entrapments of drunkenness or prostitution, but religious hypocrisy also strikes at the heart of God's reputation in the world.

The one possibility that Satan dreads is that we might discover the priceless freedom Christ purchased for us. He fears this liberty because he knows that it is only by the Spirit, by faith and not by our works, that we triumph over sin. Our freedom in Christ is a foil to all his schemes. So, Paul writes, "walk by the Spirit, and you will not gratify the desires of the flesh" (Gal. 5:16). Hear the promise implicit in that verse. Walk in freedom and faith, live in the light of the Spirit's work; don't rely on your good works, and you *will not* gratify fleshly cravings.

When I think of the "works of the flesh," I usually recall this list: "sexual immorality, impurity, sensuality, idolatry, sorcery, enmity, strife, jealousy, fits of anger, rivalries, dissensions, divisions, envy, drunkenness, orgies, and things like these" (Gal. 5:19–21). But in the four chapters prior, Paul equated the "works of the flesh" with slavery to the law, legalism, and works-righteousness. He contrasted works of the flesh and legalism with the work of the Spirit and freedom. He knew that legalistic law keeping doesn't keep sin out; it actually engenders self-indulgence and the pride that breeds conflict and competition. On the other hand, standing in our law-free faith will result in the sweet fruit of the Spirit: "love, joy, peace, patience, kindness, goodness, faithfulness, gentleness, [and] self-control" (Gal. 5:22–23).

Does that seem upside down to you? It does to me. What I think I need are more rules to live by. Give me a pen and a sticky pad, and I can get my life together. But the Spirit knows that what I need isn't more rules; it's freedom, *because the motive and power to obey is always absent in slaves.* Slaves have no hope; they resent their masters, and they will always escape if given the opportunity. On the other hand, adopted children who are freely loved will choose to serve out of astonishment at their father's generosity and their undeserved liberty. Such powerful love endues them to fight against every desire that might displease their father. Slaves don't love; children do.

My Father,

*Thank you that your Son purchased my freedom. Thank you that I'm not
only no longer enslaved to sin, but I am also freed from the law. Please illumine my understanding and show me the ways in which I rely upon law
keeping to make myself acceptable to you. And then please grant me grace to
see myself as I really am: not a manacled slave but your beloved daughter.*

AMEN

Day 18

A Broken Heart

Restore to me the joy of your salvation,
and uphold me with a willing spirit.

PSALM 51:12

There are some days when, by his good grace, God deeply strikes
my heart and shows me my sin. When God awakens me to it, it's
easy for me to despair, to believe that I'm not changed, that I'll never
change, to run. Although I know that the Lord does love me, at that
moment his love isn't the sweet cordial for my soul that it's meant to
be. It's more like lukewarm water on a blistering August day. "Yes,"
I whimper, "God does love me, but right now all I can see is what a
wretch I'm afraid I am."

I struggled through a morning just like that recently. I remembered how I had sinned against kindness, how I had wounded a
faithful heart. An aching awareness of my idolatries, hypocrisies,
self-deception, pride, and ingratitude eclipsed my love, and an ashen
blanket of hopelessness and despair settled down over my soul. I
acknowledged my sin to God, but still my heart was icy, detached,
deadened. Yes, God is good, but I knew I hadn't been, and thinking
about my sin felt too humbling.

Because I had obligations to see to, I dressed and went about my
business. As I was traveling to my appointment I thought, *I think I'll
blow off work today; I work hard, I deserve a day off. I think I'll go
shopping.* I entertained myself with the joys of a new outfit, perhaps

jeans and a spiffy new blouse. I hastily planned what stores I would visit. But somewhere between my appointment and the freeway, the Spirit gently worked in my heart. I knew that although I could go shopping, shopping wasn't what I needed to do. I went home and very slowly began a journey back toward him.

You have likely read in Psalm 51 of David's sorrow after committing adultery and murder. (Please take a moment now to read it in its entirety. I've placed it in Appendix 2 for your convenience.) David was crushed with guilt; he rightly felt the weight of his transgression. His heart was on fire with his shame, he couldn't escape his failures, and his wickedness pressed him down. "I know my transgressions, and my sin is ever before me," he agonized. "Against you, you only, have I sinned and done what is evil in your sight, so that you may be justified in your words. . . . Behold, I was brought forth in iniquity" (Ps. 51:3–5).

David recognized his poverty of soul. He had nothing to recommend him. I, too, was beginning to see my utter bankruptcy. Neither David nor I dared boast before God, "Look at all the good works I've done; don't I deserve a break?" No, the only way to progress was to let the full realization of my sin press in on me, but I fought against it and love waned. I felt overwhelmed. "I know my transgressions . . . my sin is ever before me." I knew all manner of delightful theology, but just then all I knew was my failure. With David I could survey my whole life from infancy on and say, "I was brought forth in iniquity"—nothing but sin from beginning to end.

David pled for cleansing and covering. "Purge me . . . wash me . . . hide your face from my sins . . . create in me a clean heart." I too asked for forgiveness, but only because I knew I should. I ran in and out of the Lord's presence, asking for cleansing but not really wanting to know what this particular sin meant about me. I sought vainly to justify my actions. I suspected that my sin was deeper than a few unkind words, but I wasn't willing yet to really know my heart.

David's prayer was apropos; he recognized his transgression. Mine was shallow, self-protective. He knew his sin was, in essence, a heart problem. He needed a heart that was cleansed of its idols. My prayer was weak because I really didn't want to see my heart. I had desired respect and security; I was willing to sin to get it. "Lord," I needed to learn to pray, "create a clean heart in me, too."

"Deliver me from bloodguiltiness, O God" (Ps. 51:14). David had spoken murder in arranging the death of a loyal servant so that he could cover his shame. I had spoken in an unkind way to get what I wanted—respect and security. I had been deceived by my heart into believing that what I was seeking and the way I was seeking it were good. I was ashamed of my murderous words and kept trying to cover them over with a gloss of respectability. *This really isn't all that bad, is it?* Instead, the Lord was teaching me to pray, "Deliver me, not just from the guilt of my words, but also from my evil desire for respect and security, and from my proud unwillingness to see the depth of my sin."

David prayed, "O Lord, open my lips, and my mouth will declare your praise." In my journey back to the Lord, praise for him was non-existent. I saw afresh how my zeal in worship was mainly predicated upon my approval of myself. *Oh Lord, if that's what I really am, how can I praise you?* I didn't want to praise him. I wanted to feel sorry for myself and hide behind plausible-sounding excuses. When he came walking in the garden, I was busy fabricating my new fig-leaf outfit. I wanted to scurry past the memory of my sin and get everything tidied up so that I could approve of myself again. He taught me afresh that the covering I needed necessitated shed blood. Sweat, cries, beatings, nails, substitutionary death. Nothing to be scurried past easily on my way to self-perfection. Nothing tidy. Only this gracious revelation would open my mouth to declare his praise.

"For you will not delight in sacrifice, or I would give it; you will not be pleased with a burnt offering. The sacrifices of God are a broken spirit; a broken and contrite heart, O God, you will not despise" (Ps. 51:16–17). I came to understand again that what he wanted from me was not my good record. Instead, he wanted brokenness and humility that would make me love him and my neighbor. David, too, knew that the Lord desired something more than mere outward sacrifice. Outward sacrifice is easy; it appeals to religious pride. God desires a heart that is broken with sin and humbled, and he patiently worked in mine until I was ready to surrender. Oh, the mercy of a God who will not scorn the sinner's broken heart!

My Father,

Thank you for your patience. Thank you that you continue to work in my heart with such grace and mercy. Thank you that your mercies are new every morning and that you're continually refashioning a clean heart within me. Deliver me from my loathing of true humility and give me the joy of your salvation again.

AMEN

Day 19

The World Overcome

*"In the world you will have tribulation. But take heart;
I have overcome the world."*

JOHN 16:33

The disciples didn't know it, but they had celebrated their last Passover meal together. Tenderly Jesus sought again to prepare them for what was coming. He spoke of betrayal, cowardice, death. Judas received bread from God's hand. Satan moved his pawn. Jesus commanded, "What you are going to do, do quickly" (John 13:27). And it was night (John 13:30).

But their plans had been progressing so swimmingly. Their Master had been welcomed with shouts of messianic acclaim: "Hosanna! Blessed is he who comes in the name of the Lord" (John 12:13). Palm branches were waved in exultation. Surely his coronation day had finally arrived. His disciples were enjoying him, leaning on his chest, privy to mysteries that were hidden from others. But now his words threatened to dim their elation. They began to feel it; a chill was in the air, night was encroaching. He spoke:

> "Little children, yet a little while I am with you. You will seek me, and just as I said to the Jews, so now I also say to you, 'Where I am going you cannot come.'" (John 13:33)
> "Where I am going you cannot follow me." (John 13:36)
> "The rooster will not crow till you have denied me three times." (John 13:38)

"I will no longer talk much with you, for the ruler of this world is coming." (John 14:30)

"But now I am going to him who sent me. . . . Because I have said these things to you, sorrow has filled your heart." (John 16:5–6)

"A little while and you will not see me. . . . Truly, truly, I say to you, you will weep and lament, but the world will rejoice. You will be sorrowful." (John 16:19–20)

"I am leaving the world and going to the Father." (John 16:28)

"Behold, the hour . . . has come, when you will be scattered, each to his own home, and will leave me alone." (John 16:32)

Confusion darkened their confidence. Was Jesus actually saying good-bye? But . . . but they had followed him for years, embraced him as Messiah, banked on his triumph, left family and employment. How could he tell them that they couldn't follow him?

We are so frequently misguided about God's plans. Day by day we measure our progress toward anticipated goals; we judge God's faithfulness and our performance by the proximity of the desired accomplishment. *Is everything progressing as it should? Am I getting through this rough patch? Are my kids achieving? Am I paying down my debt? Is my boss finally appreciating me?* And then the kids fail (again!); foreclosure looms; we discover that the boss not only doesn't appreciate us, but he's actually considering demoting us. *Hold on!* we think. *This isn't what I signed up for. This isn't right. I've followed God. Where is he now that I really need him? What happened to all the plans we made together?*

We suffer because we mistakenly believe that God's goals and our goals are identical. Into this confusion and sorrow, your Savior, who isn't insensible to your pain, speaks. "I have said these things to you, that in me you may have peace. In the world you will have tribulation. But take heart; I have overcome the world" (John 16:33). We think, *The fact that I'm going to have tribulation is quite obvious, thank you. And, it's nice that you've overcome the world (whatever that means), but how does that help me right now?*

The gospel dispels darkness and confusion. It tells me about him, about myself. It tells me that I am *in* him, and because that's my identity, I can have peace when peace is beyond comprehension. But my experience of peace in tribulation also grows more brightly as I remind myself of the things he taught (John 16:33). He taught these truths so that I might have peace; they shatter my misguided illusions: my selfish ambition, even for his kingdom, is not his goal. Washing feet is. I believe that a pleasant existence free from tribulation will bring me happiness. He teaches that fullness of joy is found in divesting myself of pride and idolatrous desire for pleasure, respect, and comfort.

I think that I am wise and know what's best. His plans confound the wisdom of the wisest man and flay him in the dust. I deceive myself into believing that I deserve better than this. He gently reminds me that I deserve an eternity of excruciating flame eating at my soul and separation from his Son.

Peace begins to fill my soul when I remember the truth of the gospel: I am more sinful and flawed than I ever dared believe, more loved and welcomed than I ever dared hope. I deserve less than nothing but have been given everything.

Jesus Christ *has* overcome the world. Although it seemed (and still seems) like night would eclipse the light, as though the "ruler of this world" would forever reign, the glorious radiance of the Son is seen with eyes of faith. Peace can flood our souls because our trust isn't misplaced. He has already overcome the world, and it will not triumph over him, and so, by implication, it will not triumph over us either because we are in union with him.

He resisted the sinful temptation to prove his rightful place as Lord of the universe. He perfectly fulfilled every command of the law. He willingly laid down his life in our place and permanently threw open the doors of heaven. He sent the Holy Spirit to comfort and teach us. We're not alone, we're not orphans; he hasn't deserted us. And he has overcome the world through his conquest of our final enemy, death. The resurrection speaks powerfully into our lives when it seems as though the light is about to be extinguished. But this world isn't all there is. What we're seeing right now isn't the end. The one who said, "I have overcome the world," walked through the travail of Gethsemane. He was nailed to a tree, suffered, bled, and died. But then he rose again, breaking the bands of death, and walked with his disciples *again*. He *had* overcome! And now he is ruling and overruling at the seat of power by his Father's right hand, there in flesh like mine and like yours. Does it feel like night? Be of good cheer; morning will dawn. He *has* overcome the world.

Day 20

Abide in the Vine

*"As the Father has loved me, so have I loved you.
Abide in my love."*

JOHN 15:9

The moon in her full-orbed beauty shone down upon the shadowed road as the Passover Lamb journeyed toward Gethsemane. Vineyards, illumined by her reflected light, stirred gently in the evening breeze. Barren branches that only days before appeared lifeless were putting forth new leaves at last. Fruitfulness was returning to the vineyard.

The Messiah stopped and gestured toward the silhouetted vines. He spoke, "I am the true vine, and my Father is the vinedresser" (John 15:1). Perhaps he reached down to lift up a tender shoot and entwine it so that it could rest against the branch. "Abide in me, and I in you. As the branch cannot bear fruit by itself, unless it abides in the vine, neither can you, unless you abide in me. I am the vine; you are the branches. Whoever abides in me and I in him, he it is that bears much fruit, for apart from me you can do nothing" (John 15:4–5).

I'll admit that although I'm familiar with this metaphor, it has always seemed a bit puzzling. Yes, I know that I need to *abide* in him, but exactly what does that entail? Should I pray more, relax more, obey more? What does this metaphor tell me about how to bear fruit? What can we learn from the vineyard?

When the little group stooped to survey vines under that moonlit sky, I'm sure they weren't immediately impressed with the power of the new spring growth. It was obvious that these fragile tendrils weren't supporting the mature vine. In fact, all they could do was receive life-giving nutrients from it. The True Vine spoke, "I'm the one giving life to you. You've just eaten the bread and the wine, my body and blood. My life is flowing in you. You are only little branches. Stay here. Abide in me. Let me supply all you need. I will do it all for you."

In my typical self-aggrandizing fashion, I overlook what he's saying about his being the vine. Instead I focus on what I have to do to abide. *Oh, yes, yes, I know that you're the vine, but now I've got to abide. Let's see, what should I do first?*

I overlook the truth that it's his power that births and sustains the entire plant. He's supplying all that's necessary for my growth and fruitfulness. It's his life, his purpose, his determination to be in union with me that's the central point of this teaching. This teaching isn't about what I must do. Yes, there is a command here, but it's basically a command simply to receive. What does that little stem need to do? If it stays attached to the vine, it will naturally grow into a fruit-producing branch. If it is broken off, it will die. It needs to abide.

In seeking to comprehend this teaching, we must remember the context into which Jesus was speaking. He was speaking to Israelites who knew that their nation had been referred to as the "vine." Jesus' warning came to them, "Every branch in me that does not bear fruit he [my Father] takes away" (John 15:2). He was foretelling the judgment that was coming upon those who refused to trust in God's Messiah, who continued to trust in themselves rather than in him (Rom. 11:17). Those who transfer their trust from themselves, Jew and Gentile alike, have passed from judgment into life, and by their union with him they bear fruit.

He goes on to say, "Every branch that does bear fruit he prunes, that it may bear more fruit" (John 15:2). For a moment take your focus off yourself and what you think you might need to do and rejoice in the promise inherent in this passage. Your fruitfulness is *assured*. Because your union isn't with a sickly, barren vine but rather with a robust and fertile one, you *will* produce fruit, the fruit he's ordained for you (Eph. 2:10). Again, it's not your ability to force fruitfulness that is in focus here. It's his ability to transform you into a lush and abundantly fruitful branch, drawing all your life and strength from his bounty alone.

Perhaps you are tempted to compare your fruitfulness with someone else's. You might look at that branch over there and wonder why your grapes don't seem as juicy. Or you might notice a big bunch of grapes on someone else and wonder what's wrong with you. Will you rest in the fact that the Father knows how to produce the fruit he desires in you? Instead of comparing yourself with others, will you abide in his wisdom and entrust yourself fully to this husbandman's skilled hands? He knows how to tease maximum fruitfulness out of your soul. It's not his plan to produce exactly the same harvest from every one of us. Don't be distressed; he will produce a harvest because we're in union with him. He is the true vine, and his hands are actively tending our growth.

Not only does the Father, the vinedresser, promise our growth in fruitfulness, but also the vine himself, Jesus, continually removes our unbelief and folly through his Word. As he was washing feet earlier in the evening, Jesus spoke these words: "You are clean" (John 13:10). Again he says, "Already you are clean because of the word that I have spoken to you" (John 15:3). We don't have to struggle to be sure that he is doing his work. He knows how to speak words of cleansing to us, washing us with the water of the Word. Yes, we need to continually expose ourselves to his Word, but the job of cleaning us up so that we can produce fruit is his.

Let your heart settle down into these astounding words: "As the Father has loved me, so have I loved you. Abide in my love" (John 15:9). When I look at my sin, my unproductiveness, that shriveled fruit, it's hard for me to believe that this kind of love is possible. But drink in what he says: "I've loved you with the same intensity of love that my Father has for me." What a shocking declaration of devotion and affection! Let your soul be nourished and grow strong in it.

Yes, he is calling us to a life of obedience, but it isn't an obedience that starts with our great efforts. It is an obedience that he has planted and now lovingly tends as we absorb his soul-nourishing life. Think of his love as the rays of the sun, the gentle cooling of the evening breezes, the soil rich in nutrients, the satisfying spring rain, the tender pruning. And as you remember this, remember also that you aren't alone in this field; you are eternally united to the true vine, and his fruitfulness is yours. Your obedience will grow because he's your husbandman. Rest here. Endure here. Remain here. Tarry here. Abide.

Day 21

Divestiture

*We have seen and testify that the Father has sent his Son
to be the Savior of the world.*

1 JOHN 4:14

Ionce heard it said that life is a series of divestitures. And, as much
as I militate against loss, separation, and pain, I know that it's true.
That divestiture is part of the fabric of our lives is evident by the fact
that even babies know how to say "bye-bye."

We are continually saying good-bye to those we love. We lose our
possessions, we leave cherished places, and we say good-bye again
and again. We groan when we discover that our employer is trans-
ferring us to another state. *Another move? But this was just starting
to feel like home!* Our children grow too quickly, and before we are
ready to hear it they are promising to write. Our hearts break when
we learn that our mother has Alzheimer's, and although she'll be with
us in body, the real "Mom" will leave us all too soon.

And finally that great divider, death, comes and separates us from
those we love, and the more we love, the greater our grief. Aside from
the mitigating comforts of the gospel, the level of grief we experience when we're separated from our loved ones is analogous to the
level of attachment we have toward them. Even the Jews understood
Jesus' attachment to Lazarus by his tears at the tomb (John 11:36). If
we hear that a distant relative has passed away, we might stop for a
moment or two to consider his life, but we're not grief-stricken in the

same way we would be at the loss of a beloved spouse. Deep love goes hand in hand with deep loss, and just as there is great joy in a close relationship, there is great sorrow when it ends. Yes, life is a series of divestitures, and some of them are more painful than others.

Even though we're all familiar with loss, and some losses are agonizingly grievous, we've never experienced the loss that was known in heaven when the Father sent his Son to earth (1 John 4:14). Even though we are quite familiar with separation in relationship, we can't imagine what it cost the Trinity to redeem us. Think about the Trinity: here was a relationship that was completely perfect in every way. There was an abundance of love and joy flowing in eternal reciprocity between the three members of the Godhead. Never was there a shadow of doubt about commitment, affection, honor. Complete faithfulness, complete agreement, complete self-sacrificing delight, and complete transparency forever and ever. As I said, we can't imagine what our sin cost him. We can't imagine the depth of a love that would sacrifice such joy for the good of another.

We should be astounded by the incarnation. Yes, we have to say good-bye, sometimes to those we dearly love, but none of us has ever said good-bye like this Father did to this beloved Son. The Son longed to return to his Father and chided the disciples because they didn't rejoice with him at the prospect (John 14:28). The Father and his Son were separated, and this separation was profound.

Astonishing as it was, the incarnation wasn't the most astonishing divestiture. Christ's return to the glories of heaven and enjoyment of the unhindered sight of his Father's glory was going to be delayed by another loss. On the cross, the Father would forsake the Son and pour out all his wrath upon him. We cannot imagine the horror and stripping felt by the God-man Jesus Christ when his Father poured out full wrath on him and forsook him. All he could cry was, "Why?" We cannot imagine the loss of the Father, who was "pleased" to crush the beloved one who brought him such pleasure. We've never known separation and loss like that. Thank God that we never will.

Yes, we suffer divestiture, and Jesus isn't insensible to our pain. He knows that we miss him, that we miss our loved ones. So he foretold his resurrection and ascension, not in cold theological terms but in warm assurances of devotion: "If I go and prepare a place for you,

I will come again and will take you to myself, that where I am you may be also"; "I will not leave you as orphans; I will come to you"; and "If anyone loves me, he will keep my word, and my Father will love him, and we will come to him and make our home with him" (John 14:3–4, 18, 23).

He invited us into his prayer so that we could know his heart: "Father, I desire that they also, whom you have given me, may be with me where I am" (John 17:24). Can you see how important it is to him that we be with him? Do you believe that he completely understands the losses we face? He was forsaken so that we would have the assurance that we never will be.

I'm assuming that there are some of you who are feeling the stripping even now. Your Savior wants you to know that he's walked this path ahead of you. He knows what it is to be separated from loved ones, to be tempted to sin because of fear of loss. He knows what it is to walk alone, to be misunderstood, to journey in a foreign land. He knows what it is to be fully forsaken, but he also knows what it is to be reunited to his beloved. Can you imagine what it was like when the risen Christ returned to his Father at the ascension? We've never seen a reunion like that. And now he has taken our flesh into heaven to guarantee that we'll never be separated from him again. Can you imagine what it will be like when we rise again and gaze upon his face, when we are grasped by his hand and fully see his glory?

Because of this you can take comfort in your loneliness and loss. The Savior is there with you. Yes, loneliness is difficult, primarily because we miss the land where we were born, that person who really knew us. We also miss heaven, that place where there won't be any more divestitures because he was stripped for us. Are you questioning God's love for you? Do you wonder if loneliness and loss is all there is? Hear John's testimony: "We have seen and testify that the Father has sent his Son to be the Savior of the world" (1 John 4:14). Yes, this life is a series of divestitures, but this life isn't all there is.

Day 22

The Hope of Righteousness

*Through the Spirit, by faith, we ourselves eagerly wait for
the hope of righteousness.*

GALATIANS 5:5

The scent of pine pervades our home, lights glow with golden radiance, candles flicker, presents are wrapped and stacked around the tree—at last it's Christmas morning. The families arrive and all the children rush to survey the bounty. "That big one's mine!" one giggles with glee. Another shakes his gift. "I bet this one has Legos!"

"You can't have your presents now, sweeties. Come away from the tree and eat your supper. I promise we'll open them after we're finished." A collective groan goes up from the kids as they move toward the table and the dinner they don't want to eat. How the minutes seem like days as Poppie reads a passage and prays. Then on and on the time drags as the adults eat, and children push food around their plates and wonder just how much longer this is going to take.

The adults gathered around the table aren't plagued with impatience like the children, because they have lived through this before. From the perspective of their experience, they know that the time to open presents will indeed come. But because the children are still so young, the wait seems interminable.

Paul, too, was waiting. "For through the Spirit, by faith," he wrote, "we ourselves eagerly wait for the hope of righteousness" (Gal. 5:5). Linked arm in arm with us and with his siblings throughout the ages, Paul tells us that like a little child he, too, is eagerly waiting. He's waiting for the "hope of righteousness." When I think of Paul, of his great faith and clear understanding of justification, I would suppose that he wouldn't need to wait for the hope of righteousness. As a matter of fact, I would think that he would be so assured of his justification that hope wouldn't even enter into it. But that's not what Paul tells us. He writes that he eagerly awaits its arrival.

How does Paul expect this hope of righteousness to come to him? He knew that it wasn't born through obedience to the law. The entire letter to the Galatians is a polemic against law keeping as a means of obtaining hope for right standing before God. No, hope for true righteousness is "through the Spirit, by faith." In essence, Paul is reminding us that the only hope of righteousness we have will be through the power of the Spirit, who engenders faith in our hearts. Our hope is not found through vain reliance on our ability.

Like you, I need hope today. I need hope to believe that one day I will be completely righteous. But when I survey my life, I have to admit I find that difficult to believe. My conscience is grieved and stricken by my lack of love, my pride, and my selfishness, yet even so I have a niggling sense that I'm still not being fully honest about my sin. Today, right now, I need faith to believe that I can indeed hope for righteousness. But where will faith to hope come from? Surely not from me, not from an examination of my own record. No, this faith is the result of the Spirit's work. It's only as we meditate upon the gospel's promise that the Spirit creates faith within our hearts. Yes, we can believe that complete righteousness will one day be ours. This is our hope. This is the assurance that the Spirit gently yet continually brings.

Like our sweet little children, though, we continue to wait. And, like them, because we're so limited and finite and because in light of eternity we're still so young, the days drag by like years, and we doubt that true righteousness will ever come. We're groaning within ourselves, waiting for our adoption (Rom. 8:23). We know that we are prone to wander. We feel our infidelity and groan, "When will I know true righteousness? When will I be free from this fickle heart? When will I truly love?"

While we yet await the assurance that we will, one day, be completely changed, as with our little children on Christmas morning we must be patient and hopeful. We must not give up in despair or seek to anesthetize our conscience with the shallow delights of this world. And then, even when we do give in to our wandering heart, we must remember our Father's promise. True righteousness and holiness *will* be ours.

Righteousness will be ours because our Father, the righteous judge, has promised it to us. He has promised to place a "crown of righteousness" upon our heads (2 Tim. 4:8). This righteous judge will not place the hood of a condemned criminal over our eyes, nor will our brow bleed from the crown of thorns. Instead, we will forever be adorned with the garland of righteousness. And today, right now, we can have sure hope because our crown is being "kept in heaven" and we are being "guarded" by God's power (1 Pet. 1:4–5).

What does your heart say to his wondrous assurances? Has the darkness of the hangman's hood descended over your eyes while you hopelessly await the descent into eternal punishment? Like Paul, like Luther, like the rest of us, you need hope. You need hope that this crown of righteousness will be given to you simply because of his great love. Remember that, because of love, someone else lost hope in your place. The executioner drove spikes into his wrists and ankles, the guard plunged a spear deep into his side. He has already journeyed through your descent into hell. And all your sins, even the unbelief that you feel right now, the apathy that your infidelity breeds—*all your sin*—was placed upon him. He has borne it all. What is your hope of righteousness? Only that this righteousness doesn't depend on you at all, but has been granted to you as a gift through the gospel.

Little child, your Father knows that the wait seems interminable, but that's only because you're still so young. Soon the crown of righteousness will be presented to you, and when it is placed upon your grateful brow, every shadow of doubt and despair will vanish. But for now, you're called to eagerly wait in hope. The day of your full righteousness will come.

My Father,

Thank you that although you are the judge, you are also my Father. Thank you that you have promised to keep me and to preserve my crown, undefiled and unfading until you make public my complete salvation. Holy Spirit, please grant me the hope that I need to live this day in faith and in the knowledge that one day, and probably sooner than I think, you'll place that crown of righteousness upon my head. Oh, God, keep my wandering heart and grant me faith to persevere and eagerly wait.

AMEN

Day 23

His Appearing

*Henceforth there is laid up for me the crown of righteousness,
which the Lord, the righteous judge, will award to me on that Day,
and not only to me but also to all who have loved his appearing.*

2 TIMOTHY 4:8

Almost no one noticed his first arrival. Of course, his father and mother huddled together to try to keep him warm, and a few terrified shepherds came to observe this curiosity, but the rest of Bethlehem and, yes, even the entire population of his world simply lived as they always had. They assumed that what they had always known would be what they would always know. And even among those who might have heard his mother's labored cry or been aware of his weak whimper, what of it? Of what import could a little baby be? He wasn't born in a palace; he didn't have famous parents. Business as usual, nothing this little infant of questionable descent could affect.

Even though that night is far behind us, not much has changed. Life goes on, and he is still being ignored, or worse yet, patronized. "Oh, yes, gentle Jesus, little baby in a manger, meek and mild. Sleep, little baby." If the world thinks about him at all, they see him wrapped in swaddling cloths, resting in a tidy manger. Sweet images of the Nativity flit through their mind, and they dismiss him like they would any other infant. They assume that if he is real, he'll return again in the same way that he came that first Christmas morning. But they couldn't be more mistaken.

For some, his return will be a terrifying introduction into an even more horrifying eternity. Imagine the following situation. Like everyone else, you are going through daily life, thinking that everything will continue as it always has. You are trying to get the kids to baseball practice, trying to remember to turn on the Crock-Pot before you run out the door. Suddenly, you feel a great earthquake and the sun's light is extinguished. The moon looks like blood, and the stars of the sky fall "to the earth as the fig tree sheds its winter fruit when shaken by a gale" (Rev. 6:12–13). You look up to where the heavens used to be, and you see someone whose personage had never even entered your mind: a rider on a white horse. But this isn't some mortal superhero come to save Gotham from a mad fiend. No, this is your divine judge; he is here to punish and visit retribution upon you for going about your life as though he were just another baby, just a nice holiday fable. In terror you watch as a sharp sword comes out of his mouth, and he strikes down the nations. In unbroken horror you stare hopelessly as he treads "the winepress of the fury of the wrath of God the Almighty" (Rev. 19:15–16).

What would your response be? Let me tell you what it *wouldn't* be. It wouldn't be a condescending, smug smile—"Oh, look, there's gentle Jesus, riding on a little donkey. Isn't he a nice example of how folks should get along?" No, with others you would crouch down in a cave, scratching at the dirt until your fingers bled and your nails tore off. You would hide and do something you have never done before—plead with the rocks, "Fall on us and hide us from the face of him who is seated on the throne, and from the wrath of the Lamb, for the great day of their wrath has come, and who can stand?" (Rev. 6:15–17). Smug unbelief would be instantaneously transformed into terrifying understanding.

This description of the return of the Christ is meant to fill unbelievers with a godly fear that drives them to him. It's meant to terrify those who aren't his. They won't love his appearing; they'll hate it.

Now, let me ask you: how does the thought of his appearing affect you? Did the previous description fill your heart with terror and shame or godly fear and comfort? When you see your failures and sins, do you fear that you, too, will cry to the rocks, or do you know that he has something different for you? Hear these reassuring words of the Spirit:

> Henceforth there is laid up for me the crown of righteousness, which the Lord, the righteous judge, will award to me on that Day, and not only to me but also to all who have loved his appearing. (2 Tim. 4:8)

By his grace we've been made to love his appearing. His astonishing love at Calvary has caused us to love him and overcome our fear. Yes, he is coming as a righteous judge to judge the world, but for you, he's coming as a husband with gifts. Instead of a sword, you'll get a crown. In the place of pleas for protection, you'll be filled with praise, rejoicing at the sight of the lover of your soul.

> For "yet a little while, and the coming one will come and will not delay; but my righteous one shall live by faith, and if he shrinks back, my soul has no pleasure in him." But we are not of those who shrink back and are destroyed, but of those who have faith and preserve their souls. (Heb. 10:37–39)

How shall we live now, while we await his coming? By faith alone; not faith in our ability to perform, but faith in his promise that right now we possess a record that will withstand the piercing gaze of this fierce warrior. Because we've got such a righteousness, he doesn't see us as his enemy; no, he loves us as his bride.

Are you trusting that he has given you his righteousness? Have you begun to believe that he is as good as he says he is? Then let this assurance sink deeply into your soul: you "are not of those who shrink back and are destroyed, but of those who have faith." You have been made to love his first appearing, and you will also love his second. You have been given courage to face him in faith and not shrink back. What is the difference between those who are destroyed and those who rejoice? Only faith—faith that his righteousness has been bestowed upon us.

On that dreadful, wonderful day, you will live because of his love. You won't live because you have done great works or sacrificed generously or overcome your sin victoriously. You will live by faith. Your faith might be weak; it might be the thinnest gossamer thread, but if it's attached to your Warrior-Husband, he will spin it into the most beautiful gown of righteousness. You won't need to plead for rocks to cover you; you will already have a covering that will furnish you with all you need to withstand his gaze, and you will love his appearing.

Your Savior will return for you powerfully, victoriously, lovingly. Whether he comes for you today (before you get your act together) or thirty years from now (again, before you get your act together), you'll love his appearing because you'll see how he loves you. A day will come when you will glimpse the face you have longed to see your whole life, and that face will reveal a countenance thrilled and delighted with you.

Day 24

Safe in His Care

*Then Jesus, knowing all that would happen to him,
came forward and said to them, "Whom do you seek?"*

JOHN 18:4

On this side of the fall, none of us can even imagine the relaxed and happy fellowship that Adam and Eve had with each other and with their Father. Together they recognized his footsteps in the garden, because they had run, like joyful children, to meet with him before. They anticipated his visits "in the cool of the day." They had never before felt fear because they were so very secure and protected in his love.

But then the tempter struck his hideous blow, and a sense of fear and inadequacy engulfed them. No longer innocent and unaware, they "hid themselves from the presence of the LORD God among the trees of the garden" (Gen. 3:8). Their dear Father had become the feared judge, and they hid.

We are still hiding. Hiding is what we do. We hide from everyone—from strangers, from those we love. We hide from ourselves; we hide from God. We fabricate a façade of goodness or beauty, humor or intelligence. We spend countless dollars and incalculable hours sprucing up these false fig-leaf identities. We want to look good and fool our neighbors. We cower behind bushes of prosperity; we clothe ourselves with our good deeds, one-upmanship, and name-dropping. We are none of us consistently authentic.

I recently had the opportunity to drive a Jaguar for a few days while attending a conference, and I liked clothing myself in this respectability. A parking valet went to retrieve the car for me, asking, "The Jag?" When I replied yes, a certain smugness settled down over my soul. Here is an identity that suited me very well indeed. I could have said, "Yes, it's a car I've been loaned for a few days. I actually drive an eight-year-old Jeep." But the painful truth is that I liked feeling superior, condescending. I liked pretending to be fully clothed, well-heeled, without need. I'm still hiding.

On the night that our Savior was betrayed, he spent time in a garden too. He was isolated from friends who had already begun to desert him; loneliness and desolation were drawing near. Hours were spent in agonizing prayer.

> "Father, if you are willing, remove this cup from me. Nevertheless, not my will, but yours, be done." . . . And being in an agony he prayed more earnestly; and his sweat became like great drops of blood falling down to the ground. (Luke 22:42, 44)

Time for prayer was over. The sleepy disciples were shocked to realize that all their worst fears were becoming reality. Listen to these words: "Then Jesus, knowing all that would happen to him, came forward" (John 18:4). Judas had filled the garden with bands of soldiers and officers from the chief priests and the Pharisees and with lanterns, torches, and weapons. Judas, too, was afraid.

Survey the courage of your Savior: "Then Jesus, knowing all that would happen to him, came forward." He stepped forward while his attackers hid behind their religious authority, their torches and weapons. He knew "all that would happen to him." He wasn't guessing, hoping to keep terror at bay by puffing himself up with violence or wrapping himself in a cloak of secrecy. He was fully aware of what it would mean to drink down the entire contents of the Father's cup; the bitter taste was already in his mouth.

"Whom do you seek?" he bravely asked them.

"Jesus of Nazareth," they answered.

"I am he."

They fell back in terror.

"Whom do you seek?" he asked again.

They answered as before.

"I told you that I am he. So, if you seek me, let these men go" (John 18:4–8). What a Savior we have! What a good shepherd! The wolves were circling, and he stepped forward, arms outstretched, keeping his little flock behind him. The wolves would attack; he would bear their attack himself. "Let these men go. . . . I have guarded them," he had recently prayed, "and not one of them has been lost" (John 17:12). He would continue to guard them in ways amazing and unheard of. He bravely guarded their bodies; he would even more courageously watch over and protect their souls.

Why should he do this? Weren't these the friends who had so recently slept through his hour of need? Weren't they the ones who had been arguing about who was greatest? Wouldn't they all run away from him? Wouldn't they deny, by actions and words, that they ever knew him? He would look for pity, but there was none, and for comforters, but he would find none (Ps. 69:20). He was completely alone, but his love for us made him strong.

Every one of them was filled with fear. They feared that they would lose the respect and position they had banked on, that they would suffer shame. They were terrified that they might lose their lives. They had loved listening to his teaching about laying down their lives for others, but they weren't ready yet to follow him. They loved themselves more than they loved him, and so they were filled with fear. And yet he guarded them.

His great heart was filled with love, and this love empowered him to place himself between danger and those he cherished. Even though his friends weren't worthy of his protection, of his sacrifice for them, he was determined. "Take me. Let them go." That's been his theme throughout all eternity. "Take me. Punish me. Let them go." His love for us is our guarantee that we'll make it all the way to heaven. He interposed his body between the wrath of the religious leaders and his weak disciples; he interposed his precious blood between the righteous wrath of his Father and his sinful bride. What a husband! What a Savior!

He sees your heart today. He knows what you fear and how you continue to try to take matters into your own hands and protect yourself. He sees when you cut off your enemy's ear, as Peter did, lash-ing out at those who threaten you, seeking to hurt them before they can hurt you. He sees when you flee naked into the night, hoping to hide yourself from failure, censure, disgrace, judgment. He sees when you swear that you don't know him, denying him by word or deed, afraid that you'll seem foolish or be persecuted. He knows when you fear the doctor's reports and try to ignore his voice speaking deeply, comfortingly to you. And yet he interposes himself between you and your enemies simply because he is determined not to lose one of those precious ones his Father has given to him.

Draw near to him today, won't you? He'll cover you with his strong arms and keep your soul safe. Don't hide; don't try to cover up. Just come as you are and thank him for his courageous love.

Day 25

Hope of Glory

Great indeed, we confess, is the mystery of godliness.

1 TIMOTHY 3:16

A s they wound their way quietly down into the catacombs, hidden
from the sight of their enemies, the early church secretly whispered its confession:

> *[Jesus Christ] was manifested in the flesh [the incarnation],*
> *vindicated by the Spirit [the resurrection],*
> *seen by angels,*
> *proclaimed among the nations,*
> *believed on in the world,*
> *taken up in glory [the ascension]. (1 Tim. 3:16)*

As they stood before their accusers, and as they were set aflame to
light pathways to Nero's parties and offered to beasts as amusement
for yawning masses, they recited this confession. They remembered
the incarnation, the resurrection, the testimony and witness of saints
and angels, the ascension. These mysterious gospel truths were not
merely a matter of mental assent, but they were also truths that illumined their hearts and gave them hope.

Hadn't Jesus condescended to be made like them? Hadn't he died,
and didn't we see him after he had risen? Didn't the angels and the
apostles testify to these truths? Hadn't the Spirit opened their hearts

to believe? Wasn't Christ now reigning in glory at the right hand of the Father? These truths were mysteries, to be sure, but they had been revealed to them. They had an assurance of godliness; they trusted that they weren't alone, suffering on their own, working in their own power. They had faith to persevere.

"Great indeed, we confess," Paul admitted, "is the mystery of godliness." In modern language he might say, "This is so strange; it will absolutely astound you. It will blow your mind." Paul would say that this mystery was so strange, so unexpected, simply because the gospel flies in the face of everything we know about how to become godly.

What do you think I would hear if I asked the average person on the street how to become godly? What do you suppose he would say? My guess is that most people (after I explained what *godly* means) would answer that one needs to obey the Ten Commandments or the Golden Rule. Others might talk about being nice, reading the Bible, or attending church. Perhaps serious Christians would explain how to avoid sin and embrace holy living. But the mysterious truth that motivated and enflamed the early church was that godliness wasn't about what they could or should do; it was about what Jesus had already done. It was about the incarnation, the resurrection, the ascension.

For Paul, our godliness is an accomplished fact through the gospel. No wonder he said it was a "great mystery"! It wouldn't be much of a mystery if we had been told that we could earn godliness or holiness, would it? After all, that's how our whole world works. I put in my nickel or time or effort or discipline, and I get back what I've earned. We are proud that we earn our own way; we are responsible and hard-working. We like to look at our record, compare ourselves to others, build barriers, exalt ourselves.

Through the gospel, the Father set our normal way of doing things on its head. Do you want true godliness? Stop working and believe in the incarnation, resurrection, and ascension. Understand realities as they truly are: you won't ever be able to accrue godliness by putting your trust in your ability to be good enough. No, godliness comes from believing these simple truths:

- *The incarnation.* Jesus Christ, the eternal, co-existent second person of the Trinity, became a man.
- *The resurrection.* Jesus Christ died to pay the penalty for sin and transfer his righteous record to us; then he rose again on the third day.
- *The ascension.* He is ruling even now at his Father's right hand and will come again to rescue his bride and take her to himself for all eternity.

Paul calls this kind of mysterious godliness the "obedience of faith" (Rom. 16:26). In contrast to obedience centered on our conformity to the law, understanding this obedience of faith requires the illumination of the Holy Spirit. Without the Spirit's work, this mystery just won't make any sense. We are hardwired legalists. It takes an act of God's Spirit to make us understand that we are free from the law as a means of godliness.

Why would the Father want us to embrace this godliness, this obedience of faith? So that "to the only wise God [would] be glory forevermore through Jesus Christ" (Rom. 16:27). When our focus is on our supposed godliness, our obedience through our own good works, then the glory (at least in part) goes to us. We forget about the need for a God-man; we know our sin is bad, but the cross seems an overreaction. The resurrection is nice in that it demonstrates Christ's deity, but the power of sin didn't really need to be broken so dramatically, did it? Aren't we managing pretty well on our own? The ascension tidies things up nicely, but does the Christ really need to remain encased in human form? Still interposing? Still interceding? Nothing glorifies God like the gospel.

The gospel shatters our glory-seeking and self-confidence and tells us that the godliness that pleases the Father is a mystery. If you sincerely want to be godly, *stop working and believe.* Believe that the gospel declares that we are all the same—helpless and yet so loved. We're all part of the same body and "partakers of the promise in Christ Jesus through the gospel" (Eph. 3:6).

To us, Jew and Gentile alike, God has revealed a precious mystery. What is this mystery, this obedience by faith (instead of works)? Simply this: "Christ in you, the hope of glory" (Col. 1:27). What hope of glory, of godliness, do we have? Do we have hope that one day, if we just try hard enough and make a detailed list and remember to pray and discipline ourselves, we'll be godly? No, our only hope of glory is the gospel. The incarnate, resurrected, and ascended Son of God, the Christ, *lives in us*. Christ is in us, and because he is, his godliness (the only godliness there is) is ours. This mysterious truth is the sweetest, most liberating truth you will ever know. Christ is in you; he's your hope of glory.

When those early Christians faced the chains and the beatings and felt the lick of the flame, the humiliation of the stripping, the mocking, and the persecution, they didn't assuage their breaking hearts through a rehearsal of their personal accomplishments. They remembered that God became a man; he died and rose again; he is ruling as the ascended Lord, and he is also dwelling within—their only hope of glory. What do you need to remember today? The same thing: the incarnation, the resurrection, the ascension. Believe the gospel, and although it is a mystery, godliness is yours.

Day 26

Rest

*"Come to me, all who labor and are heavy laden,
and I will give you rest. Take my yoke upon you, and
learn from me, for I am gentle and lowly in heart,
and you will find rest for your souls."*

MATTHEW 11:28–29

For forty years they wandered through the wilderness, and their destination was the grave. They weren't on their way to the land flowing with "milk and honey." They were on their way to die. Until they drew their last labored breath, they would never experience the rest that had been offered to them. Yes, they would enjoy light and warmth at night, shade during the sweltering day, and manna in the morning, but they weren't getting any closer to the land of promise. No, they were going nowhere, waiting until their bones bleached in the wilderness. Yes, they knew the simple joys of faith, of family, of provision, but these joys would never eradicate the knowledge of their destiny; they were under God's judgment. The Lord was with them, but his presence didn't change the truth: he had sworn they would not enter his rest "because of their unbelief" (Heb. 3:19).

Like us, this wandering family, the Israelites, had had the gospel preached to them. The good news had begun with Abraham: "In you all the families of the earth shall be blessed" (Gen. 12:3). It continued throughout their generations—they became a great nation (Deut. 4:7), and God multiplied them (Deut. 7:13). "It is because the LORD loves you and is keeping the oath that he swore to your fathers, that the LORD has brought you out with a mighty hand and redeemed you from the house of slavery" (Deut. 7:8). "My presence will go with you, and I will give you rest" (Ex. 33:14). This good news, these gospel words, were preached to them for hundreds of years, but it did not profit them because most of them just couldn't believe that God was that good, that loving, that powerful. They just wouldn't rest in him, in the work he had done, in the work he would do.

In relating how the Israelites failed to enter into the promised rest, the writer of Hebrews teaches us what that rest looks like. He reminds us that even God himself rested from all his work. On the seventh day of creation, the Lord observed everything he had made. His creation was good, and he enjoyed it. He ceased his work and simply gloried in himself. He had called the Israelites to do the same: "Stop thinking that you need to accomplish this great work on your own! I will make you great; I'll drive out your enemies. Believe that I love you this much and that I'm powerful enough to give this land to you. Don't be afraid; don't let your fear make you grumble and sin. I will fulfill my promises!" But they didn't believe. They wanted to stone their leaders; they charged God with wrongdoing, and they longed for the security of slavery. "In their hearts they turned to Egypt" (Acts 7:39).

We have heard the same good news. The Lord has made promises to us, too: "I love you. I have given you all you need. I will bring you into a land so full of delights you'll not be able to describe it. You'll be given a righteousness you didn't earn, a forgiveness that will remove all your sins, a future beyond all you could ask or think. Simply believe." We're called to enter into that rest, just as God entered into his rest on the seventh day: "Whoever has entered God's rest has also rested from his works as God did from his" (Heb. 4:10). What are we to do? We are to do just what God did: simply survey his wonder—his power, his grace, his mercy, his kindness, his love—and then glory in it. Rest in him.

And, surprisingly, we're to strive. But we are not to strive to work. We are to strive to do something even more difficult. We are to strive to enter into rest. "Let us therefore *strive to enter that rest*, so that no one may fall by the same sort of disobedience" (Heb. 4:11). We are to strive to turn our hearts away from the false security of slavery and toward his great work through his Son. We must strive to remind ourselves continually of the work that's already been done. If we don't, we will fall into the "same sort of disobedience" the Israelites succumbed to.

It's hard to see how lack of rest can be an act of disobedience, but it is, because fear, rebellion, self-indulgence, anger, and self-pity are bred by unbelief in the goodness of God. How do we fight against our unbelief? How do we strive to enter into rest? We silence our self-reliance, pride, and unbelief by glorying in his work on the cross.

Listen, now, to the words of your Savior:

> Come to me, all who labor and are heavy laden, and I will give you rest. Take my yoke upon you, and learn from me, for I am gentle and lowly in heart, and you will find rest for your souls. For my yoke is easy, and my burden is light. (Matt. 11:28–30)

How many times has your heart been encouraged by this gracious invitation? Oh, what a Savior we have! "Come to me," he invites. "Turn from yourself, from your own work. Do you feel your slavery? Is your soul laboring beneath the arduous burden of the law? Then come." And here's his promise: "I will give you rest." He'll free you from the self-reliance that seems so logical but is, in reality, so damning. Your salvation, your endless happiness, and your acceptance with him don't depend on you. They never did. He's done it all. Simply believe, enter into what he's done, make yourself sit down and survey the landscape: see Bethlehem, Nazareth, Calvary, Jerusalem. Take a deep breath and let the burden go. Believe and rest.

It is this rest, and this rest only, that will cause you to willingly accept his yoke. It is only from a position of rest, as a beloved daughter or son, that you will learn what it means to be his. You will see him as he is, not as a severe taskmaster, demanding what you cannot give. You will see him as he is, a gentle and lowly servant. Day after day you will see life with him as it is, a refreshing repetition of delight and joyful service. Every day with him is easy; his burdens are light because he has borne the labor. He carried the heavy burden for you. Strive today to shed the yoke of the law and believe that he is that good. Accept his invitation: "Come to me and I will give you rest."

"Yes, Lord, bind me to you, make me believe, and cause me to cease my work and to strive to enter into your rest. To you will I come."

Day 27

Controlled by Love

The love of Christ controls us, because we have concluded this:
that one has died for all, therefore all have died.

2 CORINTHIANS 5:14

"This anger of mine is so terrible! I know that God wants me to learn to control it but it's so hard! I'm afraid that if I don't stop, my kids will hate God."

"My addiction to the Internet is wrong, I know. I keep telling my husband that I'll quit and then I find myself wanting to take just a peek. Then hours and hours are consumed before I unplug. The whole time I'm on it I keep telling myself 'just one more minute.' I'm wasting so much time! I know this is a terrible witness."

"I feel like such a loser. I keep worrying about failing, so I can't concentrate on my work, and I end up getting fired. My bills are piling up. I know that this is wrong and that God wants me to get over it, but I just can't seem to."

The Christian life is a war. We are called to battle the world's deceptions, our own sinful desires, and our enemy's treachery. We're in a war, and for most of us this battle is all too close to home. We love God and we want to live lives that reflect that love. But our desire to change is often driven by other motives than just love for God. Sometimes we're motivated by a desire to be free from war—to finally and fully "get over it," whatever *it* might be—and have a little peace in our lives. At other times, we worry about how our failures will affect those we love—our spouses and children. And then, of course, there is always our pride. We hate to admit to ourselves that we're not free from the alluring power of our sin and that we fail. Perhaps for some of us, avoiding the need for such an admission is the most powerful motive of all. It's just so humiliating to have to admit that we are not the people we should be after all these years of trying.

Yes, the Christian life is a war, but it's a war fought for specific reasons. It's easy to say that we are fighting for God, but because we are so easily deceived, we'll need to dig a bit deeper. We can do so by observing our responses when we succeed and when we fail. If we are self-righteous, demanding, proud, or critical of others' failures when we succeed, then we are not fighting this war out of love for God. We are fighting out of love for ourselves, our reputation, a good report card. This pride makes us impatient and self-reliant. On the other hand, if we're self-condemning, unbelieving, and angry with ourselves when we fail, then we're fighting because we long to approve of ourselves, and we despair when we can't. No matter what our heart's motives for fighting against sin, our warfare has to be firmly rooted in the gospel, or it will quickly degenerate into hedonistic self-improvement.

The desire to change isn't exclusively Christian. Everyone, Christian and non-Christian alike, wants to change. That's why bookstores are filled with self-help books and meeting halls are filled with people trying to overcome addictions to everything from gambling to pornography to shopping. Everyone wants to get better, to approve of herself, to have the respect of others, to be mentally "healthy," to keep her family together, to learn to be productive. Christians don't usually say, "I want to approve of my record." Instead they say things like "I want to feel good about myself," or "I know that this weakness of mine doesn't please God, and I'm so embarrassed." But there's a problem here for us: self-improvement isn't a Christian construct; death and resurrection are. Paul wrote:

> For the love of Christ controls us, because we have concluded this: that one has died for all, therefore all have died; and he died for all, that those who live might no longer live for themselves but for him who for their sake died and was raised. (2 Cor. 5:14–15)

God isn't interested in self-improvement regimens. He isn't impressed by our resolutions to do better, to get those devotions in, pass out tracts, cut down on our online time by fifteen minutes every day, or fast from the shopping channels during Lent. In fact, he isn't impressed with us at all. He's impressed by his Son. He's impressed with the perfect life, death, resurrection, and ascension of Jesus the Christ, his beloved Son. He's impressed with his love.

Here's the crux of the matter: you shouldn't hope to be impressed with yourself. Dead people don't worry about impressing others. They don't worry about anything. We need resurrection. We should be utterly and entirely impressed with only this: Christ died and was raised. His love was so powerful that he bent under the cruel tree, rested himself upon it, submitted to the hammer and spike, swallowed his Father's bitter wrath, relinquished his life, and then by the power of the Spirit was raised again. All this for us! *Now there's something to be impressed with.*

When he died, he died for us. When he was raised, we were raised with him. We are living in the power of the Spirit that raised him from death. The war's been won; the victor reigns. These are the thoughts that must engage our heart. We will not be able to fight victoriously against our sins unless we fight under the banner of the gospel and thereby detach ourselves from our hedonistic plans for self-improvement. We who live in him are no longer to live for ourselves, not even for our good record, our family's approval, or our clean conscience. We are to live for him who for our "sake died and was raised" (2 Cor. 5:15).

There are thousands of reasons we want to be better people, but none of them means anything except this one: the love of Christ. When we're captivated by this love, when we are drawn by the Spirit to adore and worship him, then our hearts are properly engaged and we are prepared for the battle. When we are thus engaged, receiving and returning his love, we will understand our enemies' temptations for what they really are. The city dump doesn't tempt us to eat when we've got carte blanche at a gourmet restaurant. The Internet has no power to allure when love is incarnate before us. Our desire for respect pales into triviality in the light of Calvary's love. Our longing to approve of ourselves becomes absurd when we survey the cross, our deserved end, our undeserved resurrection. Look at the great love poured out there.

Fight, dear sister. War on, dear brother. Yes, let us march onward with the cross of Jesus, not with our desire for self-improvement, a good record, a clean conscience. Let the love of Christ control you and live no longer for yourself but rather for him who died and was raised. Live in that love and war on.

Day 28

Passed Over

"On that day there shall be a fountain opened for the house of David and the inhabitants of Jerusalem, to cleanse them from sin and uncleanness."

ZECHARIAH 13:1

Today is just like every other day. Yes, there is some commotion in the temple. Yes, there is to be an execution. But, after all, this is Jerusalem; those Romans aren't squeamish about punishing us Jews. Yet our religious leaders aren't the sort of people who let things get out of hand, especially not now, with the city so full of Passover pilgrims. Yes, this is just another day in just another city under Rome's harsh rule. Just another day, remembering our slavery in Egypt and straining to be free from our slavery to Rome. Just another day . . .

As we progress through our Passover celebrations, we recall the prophecies. But will Messiah come? Will a deliverer rescue us as Moses did so many thousands of years before? We eat the Seder meal. The youngest child asks the question, "Why is this day different from any other day?" and the rote answers are recited. This is the day we remember our deliverance from slavery. These are the days we let hope live again. But is this Passover somehow different?

Yes, we are prepared. We've chosen a young lamb for our celebration, one without blemish, three years old. We've slaughtered it, drained its blood, and painted our doorposts. We are careful not to break one bone. We will eat the meal, the lamb, the unleavened bread, the sweet wine. We will sing together, dip our bread in bitter herbs, remember our slavery, rejoice because death passed over us and struck down our enemies' beloved sons. Our tradition is beautiful; it brings us hope.

He has walked through our towns for three years. He has touched lepers, invited children to crawl up into his lap. He has invited us to come to him, and we would have, but there was that shocking saying, "You must eat my flesh and drink my blood." Our leaders warned us, "If you follow him, we'll put you out of the temple." His followers are untaught fishermen, prostitutes, tax-collectors. Surely the true Messiah wouldn't associate with such as these. We thought perhaps he was the one, but no. He is just another religious zealot in a long line of religious zealots. And now he is going to die. Oh, well. Neither we nor the Romans could have someone going around claiming to be God, claiming to be king.

But on this day, in the heart of Jerusalem's power, Pilate's jaded conscience is strangely troubled. "I find no guilt in him" (John 18:38).

"If you release this man, you are not Caesar's friend" (John 19:12).

"What have you done, Jesus? Answer me! Don't you know I have authority to punish you?"

"You would have no authority over me at all unless it had been given you from above" (John 19:11).

Yet even more troubled, Pilate sought to relieve his own distressed conscience. "When Pilate saw that he was gaining nothing, but rather that a riot was beginning, he took water and washed his hands before the crowd, saying, 'I am innocent of this man's blood; see to it yourselves.' And all the people answered, 'His blood be on us and on our children!'" (Matt. 27:24–25).

Now, in the streets, they thrust the tree upon him. He stumbles. "You don't think we're going to carry your cross for you, do you?" the soldiers mock. "This is your execution. Not ours."

"Let someone else carry it for him. We don't want him to break a bone before he climbs up The Skull."

Now on the hill. "Look at him. Hanging there, naked; a mockery. The 'I Am'? Hardly. If you're God, then come down here and prove it. Be careful not to get too near. We don't want to be defiled for the celebration."

"Here, dip this rag in bitter wine for him."

The guards receive a command, "Kill the prisoners now. These superstitious dogs don't want their land defiled by letting them hang here overnight."

"This one seems to be dead already. I will make sure."

"One of the soldiers pierced his side with a spear, and at once there came out blood and water" (John 19:34).

The beloved Lamb is beaten, mocked, cursed, pierced. How does his Father respond?

> "I will pour out on the house of David and the inhabitants of Jerusalem a spirit of grace and pleas for mercy, so that, when they look on me, on him whom they have pierced, they shall mourn." (Zech. 12:10)

Our sins call for unimaginable wrath and fury. We're religious; we delight in our traditions. We love feeling chosen, righteous, separate from Gentile scum. Yes, pass the bread, answer the questions, remember the deliverer, feel good. But we're also Roman oppressors. We, too, relish opportunities to mock the weak and scorn sufferers. We gleefully watch as this man Jesus stumbles down the street. We would have enjoyed taking a crack at him, too.

Our sins call for unimaginable wrath and fury. How does he respond? Will he pour out wrath? No, he pours out a spirit of grace and mercy. Grace and mercy for us all—for Jew and Gentile—to repent. "Why is this day different from any other day?" Because we have seen our sin and been given grace to repent.

On this day, this marvelously different day, *God* applies the blood to the doorposts of our souls. This precious blood springs from the fountain in his Son's bleeding side. Again he sees blood. Again he passes over his chosen ones.

We haven't prepared for this. Our souls are full of self-righteousness, our hearts infected with leaven; our consciences have grown callous. We aren't really looking, waiting, hoping for our Deliverer. We're simply enjoying our traditions, living each day as it comes to us.

> On that day there shall be a fountain opened for the house of David and the inhabitants of Jerusalem, to cleanse them from sin and uncleanness. (Zech. 13:1)

On this day in Jerusalem a fountain has been opened for Jew and Gentile alike. It flows and flows, on and on, from his pierced side and covers over all our sin. It covers our religious sin. It covers our irreligious sin. In one stroke, the Father has opened this fountain and with it he washes away all our sin and uncleanness. Our souls are cleansed by this water, atoned for by this blood. He opens a fountain that will never run dry; this well is sufficient for us all. We have pierced him. He has taken that blood and water and made us his own.

Dear friend, the day you are facing may seem like any other day: uneventful, business as usual, nothing to celebrate. But ask yourself, *what makes this day different from any other day?* Then look on him whom we have pierced and remember, there is a fountain opened to cleanse you from all your sin and uncleanness. "For Christ, our Passover lamb, has been sacrificed. Let us therefore celebrate" (1 Cor. 5:7–8). Yes, let us celebrate this day that is different from every other day. Let us celebrate Christ, our Passover Lamb, today.

Day 29

Draw Near

Let us draw near with a true heart in full assurance of faith,
with our hearts sprinkled clean from an evil conscience
and our bodies washed with pure water.

HEBREWS 10:22

How many times have you heard sermons about prayer that have left you feeling guilty? Sometimes sermons on prayer make us determined to pray more. And if prayer is something you struggle with, it is likely that each time you hear such a sermon, you hope that this will be the one that will finally help.

How many times have you wondered why you don't enjoy prayer, thinking there must be something intrinsically wrong with you, something that makes you different? How many books have you read on prayer and how many prayer formulas have you embraced? How many times have you wondered why other saints seemed to enjoy something you find so tedious?

Yes, it's true; most of us struggle to pray. We struggle to pray for at least two reasons, both of which have their genesis in failure to believe the gospel. The first reason we don't pray is that we don't really think we need to. Unless we are in an especially difficult trial, we are pretty satisfied in our self-sufficiency. "Give us this day our daily bread"? Why would we need to pray that? We've got our savings account and our paycheck from work, and the cupboards are overflowing. "Deliver us from evil"? Yes, we suppose we should pray those words, but it seems like we are really doing a pretty good job delivering ourselves because, after all, we are resisting those big sins.

We are confirmed in our self-sufficient blindness, convinced that we are doing okay. We don't believe that we are as sinful and weak as God says we are. We feel pretty strong; we are making it. We function like unbelievers.

So we give a nod to prayer and think we are fulfilling our duty to a God who tells us we should pray, without ever really feeling our great need for prayer. Prayer is our way of silencing our nagging conscience. It's more about us than about him. It's our way of saying please and thank you to a rich but distant uncle who controls the purse strings and demands the quarterly letter. We've got to keep those checks coming in, so we write the letter and hope we have said enough. "Whew," we think, after saying our *amen*. "Got that done. Now on to the real business of the day. Where's that list got to?"

The second reason we have little fervor in prayer is that we are not really very comfortable in God's presence. We suppose that he is sitting up in heaven wishing we would get our act together. We recall our stubborn prayerlessness. We are afraid that we resonated too strongly with the last paragraph. We suspect that God knows we are just "doing our duty." He knows we are trying to snow him and that we are just looking out for ourselves. He knows that we are having trouble convincing ourselves that we really want to pray, and our guilt makes us uncomfortable with him. Prayer makes us feel like we have been called into the principal's office and that we'll have to sit there and try to think of the right answers while he shakes his head and asks, "How many times have I told you . . . ?"

Yes, we believe the gospel, but only to a certain extent. We concede that we're sinful and flawed, but we are not really desperate. We acknowledge that he has loved and welcomed us, but we are not ravished by that fact. We believe, but we function like unbelievers. Only gospel truths can make us love to pray. Only gospel truths are powerful enough to trounce our intractable self-sufficiency. We enter the holy places only "by the blood of Jesus" (Heb. 10:19). We can't come in (even if we wanted to) through our own good efforts.

No; in fact, our hypocritical good efforts performed to appease God are merely one more devious strategy deployed to avoid Jesus

Christ. Think of this: he groaned on the tree under the weight of our self-righteousnesses. He paid the penalty for them. We enter in only with blood. Only God's blood can overcome our sin. It took the tearing of the curtain that separated the holiness of God from the sinfulness of man to make a way for us to enter. What was this torn curtain? It was the true flesh of the incarnate Son of God (Heb. 10:20).

We are not desperate to pray, because we are self-deceived. We are blind to our depravity. We don't see ourselves as we really are. Do you want to learn to pray more? Learn of your sin. Ask him to show it to you, to give you a glimpse of your need. Ask him to show you what your sin cost him. Look at the cross again and again until you can say, "Lord, I'm so sinful, so weak, so deceived. Please, God, don't let a day go by without reminding me of this. Make me dependent."

Only gospel truth can make you love to pray. Only the gospel can assure my trembling heart. But we can face this reality of our sin, our independence, and our pride and then want to be near him because "we have a great priest" (Heb. 10:21). This high priest has taken our flesh and his shed blood into the very presence of his Father and now stands there, with us. This kind of love and substitution is unbelievable. Without the work of the Spirit, no one could believe it. The coexistent, coequal, eternal Son of God, who is spirit, took to himself a body, and he continues to bear it. He interposes his scars, he raises his hands. He says, "Father, forgive them." The Father looks with love and delight upon his Son and his Son's bride. He loves the bride as he loves the Son. The bride is his beloved because she belongs to his Son. She bears his resemblance; he bears hers. As the great priest that he is, he has made atonement for all her sin. The Father's heart bursts with joy and delight. The Son embraces her as his dearly loved bride.

Only the gospel will make you comfortable with the bridegroom. Only the gospel will warm your affections so that you will long for an opportunity to be near him, to rest your head on his breast, to feel the warmth of his nearness, to let him put his arm around your drooping shoulders and say, "I'm here. You're mine. Soon these interposing years will end, and your faith will be sight. Stay here by me for a while and let me give you my strength. See how I love you."

Let the gospel, and only the gospel, motivate you to prayer. Put aside your desire to approve of yourself and your fear of his disapproval. Simply flee to him. "Let us draw near with a true heart in full assurance of faith" (Heb. 10:22). Draw near; know that you have needed cleansing but have been cleansed. Know that you have deserved wrath but have been fully loved. Sit down with your beloved and hear him speak to you. Unburden your heart before him. Have fellowship with your heavenly husband. Be fully assured: he loves you when you pray, and he loves you when you don't. You're his bride when you hide from him, when you ignore him, when you think he doesn't really care. Run, now, to the lover of your soul.

Day 30

Sit Down and Believe

*We are treated as impostors, and yet are true; as unknown,
and yet well known; as dying, and behold, we live; as punished,
and yet not killed; as sorrowful, yet always rejoicing; as poor,
yet making many rich; as having nothing, yet possessing everything.*

2 CORINTHIANS 6:8–10

Morning turned to afternoon and still the crowds that followed this rabbi pressed on. Yes, they were far from home and it was true that they had finally eaten the last of their meager provisions, but still, they couldn't turn away. Yes, they were hungry and tired, but there was something here that made them stay on, even though it seemed foolish to do so. They had seen him heal the sick. They had heard his teaching and learned truths that both comforted and disturbed them. Like sheep in the field, they anxiously milled around, listened to the latest tales of his work, wondered if this was finally the king that would deliver them from Rome. But there was also that gnawing hunger, and they were well past the point of no return. What would they do now? What could they do? They had nothing, no corner market, no ATM card, no government services for the homeless. They were devoid of any answer to their dilemma.

Jesus asked his disciple, "Where are we to buy bread, so that these people may eat?" (See John 6:1ff.) Philip looked at the crowd and determined that even if they could work for two hundred days, it would not be enough to feed such a group. Feed all these? Philip knew they didn't have the resources, no matter how hard they worked. Andrew piped up. "There's a boy here with five barley loaves and two fish, but what are they for so many?" Compared to the need, these little loaves and two fish were nothing. "What are they for so many?" The need was too great. The resources too small. They weren't able to labor hard or long enough to feed this crowd. Passover was upon them and they had nothing—nothing, that is, aside from the incarnate bread of life.

"Have the people sit down," Jesus commanded. Then the thousands ate and were satisfied. Now, "gather up the leftover fragments" (John 6:10, 12). The people had been hungry, unable to find food. They would have worked, but there was no work to be had that could satisfy such a great need. The Messiah spoke: "Have the people sit down."

Like them, we too, have nothing. We have no innate goodness, no righteousness, no wisdom, no strength, no miraculous power to enable us to work hard enough to meet the overwhelming need of our souls. We are completely bankrupt; we're devoid of the power we need to conquer our sin, to change our nature. We have exhausted all our supplies, and although we are willing to work (in fact, we'd prefer to), there is just nothing that we can do that will satisfy such a wretchedness. We are starving for true righteousness, hungering to be able to meet God's standards, languishing as we try to satisfy the ever-growing needs of those around us. We have nothing of our own. But our Savior calls to us, "Sit down."

He tells us, "Do not labor for the food that perishes, but for the food that endures to eternal life, which the Son of Man will give to you" (John 6:27). Ah, good, we think. Now he's going to tell us how we can earn our way. "Yes, Lord, we think. We're ready to labor. Just tell us, 'What must we do, to be doing the works of God?'" (v. 28).

"This is the work of God, that you believe in him whom he has sent" (v. 29). His answer to our prayer for some labor to do is to sit down and believe. That's all the work we can do. And he will give us eternal life. "I am the bread of life," he said. "Whoever comes to me shall not hunger, and whoever believes in me shall never thirst" (v. 35).

It is true that, as Paul testified, we have nothing (2 Cor. 6:10). We have nothing to recommend us, no works we can do to make our situation better, no riches to donate, no wisdom with which to instruct him. In fact, we have less than nothing; we're in debt. So our Savior calls us to do the one thing we can all do: "Sit down. . . . Believe."

Yes, it's true that we have nothing. Recognizing our innate destitution and bankruptcy is so freeing. It so strips us of self-reliance that our busy heart is able, at last, to find calming rest. It tells us that what we need to do is stop milling about, trying to find something we can do to make ourselves better. All we can do is sit down and trust that he is handling it. He's got lunch covered. He's got eternity covered. He's got our sin covered. All we can do is sit down and let him serve us. Amazing condescension and grace.

But our destitution isn't all there is. Paul described his life with these words: "as having nothing, yet possessing everything" (2 Cor. 6:10). Not only do we have nothing, but we also possess everything. We've been given more than an abundance of blessing—not just a scrap or two of bread, not just a bite of fish. There is an abundance, there is plenty, there are leftovers. When Jesus serves you, expect to be overwhelmed.

Let me help you unpack a portion of the feast he has prepared for you. Here are a few thoughts to feed your soul:

- He loved you and chose you before the earth was created (Eph. 1:4).
- Even though you were intentionally fighting against him as his enemy, he loved you and intentionally died in your place (Rom. 5:10).
- You have been completely absolved of all your sins, even those you have yet to commit (Col. 1:14).
- The record of all your sin has been obliterated (Col. 2:14).
- The record of his perfect life has been applied to you (2 Cor. 5:21).
- His Father has permanently adopted you as a beloved child (Eph. 1:5).
- He has placed his Spirit within you as a guarantee that you will persevere (Eph. 1:13).
- He is guarding you every moment of every day (1 Pet. 1:5).
- He is faithful to care for you even in the midst of trials (1 Cor. 10:13).
- One day you will take your first step into light, and that eternal journey will bring you more joy and blessing than you can ever imagine (Ps. 16:11).

In the light of this wonderful repast, let me encourage you to put aside the rotting lunch you have brought along for yourself. Your own righteousnesses, your own "good record," your own faithfulness is simply putrid garbage in comparison to this. Feast here, drink here; nourish your soul. In him you possess all things. Jesus is serving you; come to him. He calls to you. "I am the bread of life; whoever comes to me shall not hunger, and whoever believes in me shall never thirst" (John 6:35). Sit down; eat, drink, believe.

Day 31

The Tree of Life

He said, "Who told you that you were naked?
Have you eaten of the tree of which I commanded
you not to eat?"

GENESIS 3:11

The voice grew closer. "Where are you?" The timorous reply
was barely heard. "I was afraid because I was naked, so I hid
myself."

"Who told you that you were naked? Have you eaten of the tree
of which I commanded you not to eat?" (Gen. 3:11).

Fear and shame engulfed their souls. Punishments were meted
out. The man would experience grinding, frustrating labor; every
ounce of fruit would cost him in sweat and blood. The woman would
suffer great pain in childbirth; her children would bring her sorrow.
Her marriage would be dissatisfying; she would chafe against her husband's rule. The snake would eat dirt and be despised. Their beautiful
garden home would be left behind as they made their way out—out
of their perfect paradise into our world. The pathway that led back
to the tree of life would be barred to them. The Lord "drove out the
man, and . . . he placed the cherubim and a flaming sword that turned
every way to guard the way to the tree of life" (Gen. 3:22). There
was no way back; they would never find that path again. Paradise
had been lost.

On this side of the fall, we cannot possibly imagine what was lost on that day. To have been perfectly cared for and perfectly protected and to enjoy unhindered communion with one another and with their Creator is a life we cannot possibly comprehend. They lived without consciousness of sin; they never experienced want, hunger, pain, shame, greed, anger, or self-pity. They were completely free and unhindered in both desire and ability. Afterward did they turn around and try to get a glimpse of the tree they had shunned? Did the radiance of the flaming sword simply serve to illuminate their shame and sorrow?

They took nothing with them. The clothing they had fashioned to hide their nakedness was stripped from them. The Lord God killed animals to cover them. They were clothed in skins fashioned by the hand of God, skins of animals that had once been in their care. An animal had cried out; his skin had been peeled from him and sewn to cover their bodies. Death, blood, and separation now infected all they knew. "Go out now, covered in the blood of another. You deserve to die; you deserve to be shamed, but I have covered you." They left the garden that had been their perfect home. They had only each other, only the skins for covering, and one promise.

They left the garden for the wilderness. They had never before had to worry about where to sleep, how to protect themselves from the elements, how to kill animals for food. The garden along with God's presence, sweet communion, and peaceful freedom from self-awareness were gone. All they had to hang onto was that one pronouncement the Lord had made to the serpent, . . . "Her offspring shall bruise your head, and you shall bruise his heel" (Gen. 3:15).

Much later, a child was born. His mother's blood was gently wiped away. He was wrapped in rough cloths, laid in a feeding trough. He whimpered; Mary sought to comfort him.

His parents were Adam's children, wilderness wanderers. They suffered under the curse meted out so many thousands of years ago. The road back to the tree of life was closed. Adam had been clothed with skins; now, the Son of God was clothed in Adam's flesh.

The Son of God was led into the wilderness. He was tempted to labor to provide for himself. "If you are the Son of God, command these stones to become loaves of bread," but he replied, "Man shall not live by bread alone, but by every word that comes from the mouth of God" (Matt. 4:3–4). Unlike his sister and brother, he refused to eat. He had heard that deception before; he had come to reverse the curse it had brought.

Later still he was led into the courtyard. The wandering soldiers looked forward to some amusement, something to ease the pain, distract them from guilt. "Strip the rough rags from him. Let's have some fun with this Jew!" The lash peeled away his skin. Blood rose to the surface and wet his back. "He says he's a king. Let's make a crown for him!" The thorns pierced his brow.

He was led up Golgotha. "Here, let's put him on this cross. Be sure you fasten him securely. It's such a bother to have to hammer those spikes in again." He was lifted up between heaven and earth. The waiting began. "I have some dice. Let's see who the lucky one will be who gets his clothing."

"Father, forgive them, for they know not what they do" (Luke 23:34).

He was covered in blood. His eyes were closed. Another took him down. He washed the blood from him. He wrapped his body in rough rags. He laid him in a tomb. He left the garden to celebrate the feast.

"Sir, if you have carried him away, tell me where you have laid him, and I will take him away" (John 20:15). Mary had loved him in life; she would care for him in death.

"Mary."

He didn't need her to take care of him. He would care for her. He was the door. He had opened the way back to life.

"Rabboni!"

He was leaving them again. He had accomplished it all. The flaming sword had been thrust into his side. It was hidden there forever. The Lamb had been slain and had risen again. And "as they were looking on, he was lifted up, and a cloud took him out of their sight" (Acts 1:9).

We are all the same. We have plucked fruit from that forbidden tree. We have proudly declared that we know best, that we can take care of ourselves. We have crowned ourselves deities. "Have you eaten from the tree?" Oh, yes and yes, over and over again in ways both glaring and hidden.

But the God-man has been slain. The Lamb's blood has been spilt, and it covers us. Our rags have been replaced with his robes. The garden has been reopened; we've been invited back in. "Here, eat of this, it will give you life."

As we celebrate our last day together, please answer these questions: Have you eaten from that tree today? Have you satiated your soul with the luscious fruit that grows from this blood-soaked ground? Have you nourished your heart with his strength, his righteousness, his perfection, and the gospel? Have you shunned self-righteousness, self-reliance, self-improvement? *Which tree are you most aware of?*

Eat from the blessed tree, dear friend. Eat and eat and never stop. When you are hungry for something else, something more, something new, run to that tree. Stay there; rest in his shade. The door is open; the meal is ready. Sit down and eat.

Appendix 1

The Most Important Good News

I didn't begin to understand the gospel until the summer before my twenty-first birthday. Although I had attended church from time to time in my childhood, I'll admit that it never really transformed me in any significant way. I was frequently taken to Sunday school where I heard stories about Jesus. I knew, without really understanding, the importance of Christmas and Easter. I remember looking at the beautiful stained glass windows, with their cranberry red and deep cerulean blue, with Jesus knocking on a garden door, and having a vague sense that being religious was good. But I didn't have the foggiest understanding of the gospel.

When adolescence came barging in, my strongest memories are those of despair and anger. I was consistently in trouble, and I hated everyone who pointed that out. There were nights when I prayed that I would be good or, more specifically, that I would get out of whatever trouble I was in and do better, only to be disappointed and angered by the failures of the following day.

Upon graduation from high school at seventeen, I got married, had a baby, and was divorced—all before the third decade of my life began. It was during the following months and years that I discovered the anesthetizing effects of drugs, alcohol, and illicit relationships. Although I would have been known as a girl who liked to party, I was utterly lost and joyless, and I was beginning to know it.

I can remember telling a friend once that I felt like I was fifty years old, which, at that point in my life, was the oldest I could imagine anyone being. I was exhausted and disgusted, so I decided to set about improving myself. I worked a full-time job, took a full load at a local junior college, and cared for my son. I changed my living arrangements and tried to start over. I didn't know that the Holy Spirit was working in my heart, calling me to the Son. I just knew that something had to change. Don't misunderstand—I was still living a shamefully wicked life; it's just that I felt as though I was beginning to wake up to something different.

At this point, Julie entered my life. She was my next-door neighbor and she was a Christian. She was kind to me and we became fast friends. She had a quality of life about her that attracted me, and she was always talking to me about her Savior, Jesus. She let me know that she was praying for me and would frequently encourage me to "get saved." Although I'd had that Sunday school training, what she had to say was something completely different from what I'd ever remembered hearing. She told me I needed to be born again.

And so, on a warm night sometime in June of 1971, I knelt down in my tiny apartment and told the Lord that I wanted to be his. At that point, I didn't really understand much about the gospel, but I did understand this: I knew I was desperate, and I desperately hoped that the Lord would help me. That prayer on that night changed everything about me. I remember it now, thirty-seven years later, as if it were yesterday.

In the words of Scripture, I knew I needed to be saved, and I trusted that Jesus could save me. One man who came in contact with some of Jesus' followers asked this same question: "What must I do to be saved?" The answer was simple: "Believe in the Lord Jesus, and you will be saved."

Very simply, what do you need to believe and know in order to be a Christian? You need to know that you need salvation, help, or deliverance. You must not try to reform yourself or decide that you are going to become a moral person so that God will be impressed. Because he is completely holy, that is, perfectly moral, you have to give up any idea that you can be good enough to meet his standard. That is the good bad news. It's bad news because it tells you that you are in an impossible situation, one that you cannot change. But it's also good news because it will free you from endless cycles of self-improvement that end in ultimate failure.

You also need to trust that what you're unable to do—live a perfectly holy life—he's done for you. This is the good news. This is the gospel. Basically the gospel is the story of how God looked down through the corridors of time and set his love on his people. At a specific point, he sent his Son into the world to become fully like us. This is the story you hear about at Christmas. This baby grew to be a man, and after thirty years of obscurity he began to show the people who he was. He did this by performing miracles—healing the sick, raising the dead. He also demonstrated his deity by teaching people what God required of them and continually foretelling his coming death and resurrection. And he did one more thing: he claimed to be God.

Because of his claim to be God, the leading religious people, along with the political powers of the day, passed an unjust sentence of death upon him. Although he had never done anything wrong, he was beaten, mocked, and shamefully executed. He died. Even though it looked like he had failed, the truth is that this was God's plan from the very beginning.

His body was taken down from the cross and laid hastily in a rock tomb in a garden. After three days, some of his followers went to properly care for his remains and discovered that he had risen from the dead. They actually spoke with him, touched him, ate with him. This is the story that we celebrate at Easter. After another forty days, he was taken back up into heaven, still in his physical form, and his followers were told that he would return to earth in just the same way.

I told you that there were two things you need to know and believe. The first is that you need more significant help than you or any other human person could ever supply. The second is that if you believe that Jesus, the Christ, is the person who will supply that help, and if you come to him, he will not turn his back on you. You don't need to understand much more than that, and if you really believe these truths, your life will be transformed by his love.

Below I've written out for you some verses from the Bible. As you read them, you can talk to God, just as though he were sitting right by you (because his presence is everywhere!) and ask him for help to understand. Remember that his help isn't based on your ability to perfectly understand or anything that you can do. If you trust him, he has promised to help you, and that's all you need to know for now.

> For all have sinned and fall short of the glory of God. (Rom. 3:23)
>
> For the wages of sin is death, but the free gift of God is eternal life in Christ Jesus our Lord. (Rom. 6:23)
>
> For while we were still weak, at the right time Christ died for the ungodly. For one will scarcely die for a righteous person—though perhaps for a good person one would dare even to die—but God shows his love for us in that while we were still sinners, Christ died for us. (Rom. 5:6–8)
>
> For our sake he made him to be sin who knew no sin, so that in him we might become the righteousness of God. (2 Cor. 5:21)
>
> If you confess with your mouth that Jesus is Lord and believe in your heart that God raised him from the dead, you will be saved. For with the heart one believes and is justified, and with the mouth one confesses and is saved. For the Scripture says, "Everyone who believes in him will not be put to shame." . . . The same Lord is Lord of all, bestowing his riches on all who call on him. For "everyone who calls on the name of the Lord will be saved." (Rom. 10:9–13)
>
> Whoever comes to me I will never cast out. (John 6:37)
>
> Therefore, if anyone is in Christ, he is a new creation. The old has passed away; behold, the new has come. (2 Cor. 5:17)
>
> Come to me, all who labor and are heavy laden, and I will give you rest. Take my yoke upon you, and learn from me, for I am gentle and lowly in heart, and you will find rest for your souls. (Matt. 11:28–30)
>
> There is therefore now no condemnation for those who are in Christ Jesus. (Rom. 8:1)

If you'd like to, you might pray a prayer something like this:

Dear God,

I'll admit that I don't understand everything about this, but I do believe these two things: I need help and you want to help me. I confess that I'm like Elyse and I've pretty much ignored you my whole life, except when I was in trouble or just wanted to feel good about myself. I know that I haven't loved you or my neighbor, so it's true that I deserve to be punished and really do need help. But I also believe that you've brought me here, right now, to read this page because you are willing to help me and that if I ask you for help, you won't send me away empty-handed. I'm beginning to understand how you punished your Son in my place and how, because of his sacrifice for me, I can have a relationship with you. Father, please guide me to a good church and help me understand your Word. I give my life to you and ask you to make me yours.

IN JESUS' NAME, AMEN

What you find in this little devotional will comfort you and help you understand more about this wonderful salvation Jesus Christ has purchased for you.

Here are two more thoughts. In his kindness, Jesus established his church to encourage and help us understand and live out these two truths. If you know that you need help and you think that Jesus is able to supply that help, or if you're still questioning but want to know more, please search out a good church in your neighborhood and begin to make relationships there. A good church is one that recognizes that we cannot save ourselves by our own goodness and that relies wholly on Jesus Christ (and no one else) for this salvation. You might call around and ask these questions or even go on the Internet to get a listing of churches in your area. Usually churches have something called a "Statement of Faith" on their Web site, which will tell you something about them.

Mormons and Jehovah's Witnesses are not people from Christian churches, and they do not believe in the gospel (though they might tell you that they do), so you don't want to go there. Finding a good church is sometimes quite a process, so don't be discouraged if you don't succeed right away. Keep trying and believing that God will help you.

Second, another factor that will help you grow in this new life of faith is to begin to read what God has said about himself and about us in his Word, the Bible. In the New Testament (the last one-third or so of the Bible), there are four Gospels, or narratives, about the life of Jesus. I recommend that you start with the first one, Matthew, and then work your way through the other three. I also recommend that you purchase a good modern Bible translation, such as the English

Standard Version, but you can get any version that you're comfortable with (although avoid what is called a *paraphrase*) and begin reading more right away.

The last request that I have of you is that you contact me through my Web site, www.elysefitzpatrick.com, if you have decided through reading this book that you want to follow Jesus. Thank you for taking time to read this little explanation of the most important good news you will ever hear.

Appendix 2

Psalm 51

Have mercy on me, O God,
according to your steadfast love;
according to your abundant mercy
blot out my transgressions.
Wash me thoroughly from my iniquity,
and cleanse me from my sin!

For I know my transgressions,
and my sin is ever before me.
Against you, you only, have I sinned
and done what is evil in your sight,
so that you may be justified in your words
and blameless in your judgment.
Behold, I was brought forth in iniquity,
and in sin did my mother conceive me.
Behold, you delight in truth in the inward being,
and you teach me wisdom in the secret heart.

Purge me with hyssop, and I shall be clean;
wash me, and I shall be whiter than snow.
Let me hear joy and gladness;
let the bones that you have broken rejoice.
Hide your face from my sins,
and blot out all my iniquities.
Create in me a clean heart, O God,
and renew a right spirit within me.

Cast me not away from your presence,
    and take not your Holy Spirit from me.
Restore to me the joy of your salvation,
    and uphold me with a willing spirit.

Then I will teach transgressors your ways,
    and sinners will return to you.
Deliver me from bloodguiltiness, O God,
    O God of my salvation,
    and my tongue will sing aloud of your righteousness.
O Lord, open my lips,
    and my mouth will declare your praise.
For you will not delight in sacrifice, or I would give it;
    you will not be pleased with a burnt offering.
The sacrifices of God are a broken spirit;
    a broken and contrite heart, O God, you will not despise.

Do good to Zion in your good pleasure;
    build up the walls of Jerusalem;
then will you delight in right sacrifices,
    in burnt offerings and whole burnt offerings;
    then bulls will be offered on your altar.

Personal Reflections

Personal Reflections

Personal Reflections

Personal Reflections

Personal Reflections

Personal Reflections